iPhone User Interface Cookbook

A concise dissection of Apple's iOS user interface design principles

Cameron Banga

PUBLISHING

BIRMINGHAM - MUMBAI

iPhone User Interface Cookbook

First published: November 2011

Production Reference: 1171111

Published by Packt Publishing Ltd.
Livery Place
35 Livery Street
Birmingham B3 2PB, UK.

ISBN 978-1-84969-114-7

www.packtpub.com

Cover Image by Asher Wishkerman (a.wishkerman@mpic.de)

Credits

Author

Cameron Banga

Reviewers

Daria Bernabei

Robb Lewis

Chris Zaplatosch

Acquisition Editor

Steven Wilding

Development Editor

Maitreya Bhakal

Technical Editor

Aaron Rosario

Project Coordinator

Vishal Bodwani

Proofreader

Aaron Nash

Indexer

Monica Ajmera Mehta

Graphics

Valentina D'silva

Production Coordinator

Alwin Roy

Cover Work

Alwin Roy

About the Author

Cameron Banga is an iOS application interface designer and entrepreneur, having played a role in the development of over 35 applications for the iPhone and iPad since beginning work on the platform in May 2009. Cameron can be found on Twitter at @cameronbanga, or at her personal website, `http://cameronbanga.com`. He can be e-mailed at `Cameron@ CameronBanga.com`.

Currently Cameron is lead designer at 9magnets LLC, which is an iPhone and iPad application design, development, and marketing studio he co-founded in May of 2010.

The team has seen strong success in the App Store and has had their work featured and reviewed positively by the New York Times, Chicago Sun-Times, Fox Business News, Macworld, PC Magazine, and more.

I'd like to thank Nathan, Mom, and Dad, thanks for putting up with my hectic schedule while remaining to be the best family a guy could ever ask for, as I can't even begin to describe my appreciation.

Kathryn, thanks for the patience and believing in me throughout this entire process, I owe you an omelet.

Adam, Aviral, Bud, Harry, Hayson, Mike, and Tom, I apologize for being the non-existent friend over the past year. To Lank 5 South, this one is for Cardboard Mike Lucien.

I'd like to give a special thanks to Maitreya, Vishal, Aaron, Steven, and the rest of the Packt Pub team, for helping direct and lead the production of this book. Thanks as well to Chris, Daria, and Robb for their unbelievably valuable feedback during the technical review stage.

About the Reviewers

Ever since the early days at the Graphic Design school in Italy, **Daria Bernabei** knew her real passion was the web. After working for several small studios, Daria moved to Barcelona and soon started to work for `lastminute.com`, where user experience and the marketing departments worked hand in hand to deliver campaigns where eye-catching creativity was balanced with high technical skill to provide adequate support on the platform side.

At the moment she leads the User Experience department in Gsicommerce International, coordinating the creation of user interfaces for online stores. Her goal is to optimize design as well as technical implementation according to the web standards and the main focus is about improving the user's shopping experience.

She is fascinated by the new challenges and opportunities that mobile devices are bringing to the web developers and a total fanatic of Apple gadgets.

Robb Lewis is a web developer and student studying web technologies at Portsmouth University. Robb has a great interest in technology, specifically mobile technology, and is an Apple advocate. Robb also blogs about software, technology, and the Internet at `http://therobb.co.uk`.

Chris Zaplatosch works in the technical support industry, specializing in customer support and management. He has more than five years of experience in the IT support field.

Since March 2011 he has been working for Blackboard Inc. as a Technical Support Manager, providing support for system administrators.

Prior to working at Blackboard, Chris spent three years working at a university help desk as a Help Desk Manager, supporting students, faculty, and staff in day to day technical operations.

Chris has a bachelor's degree in Business Management from Valparaiso University.

www.PacktPub.com

This book is published by Packt Publishing. You might want to visit Packt's website at
`www.PacktPub.com` and take advantage of the following features and offers:

Discounts

Have you bought the print copy or Kindle version of this book? If so, you can get a massive
85% off the price of the eBook version, available in PDF, ePub, and MOBI.

Simply go to `http://www.packtpub.com/iphone-user-interface-cookbook/book`,
add it to your cart, and enter the following discount code:

ipuicebk

Free eBooks

If you sign up to an account on `www.PacktPub.com`, you will have access to nine
free eBooks.

Newsletters

Sign up for Packt's newsletters, which will keep you up to date with offers, discounts, books,
and downloads.

You can set up your subscription at `www.PacktPub.com/newsletters`

Code Downloads, Errata and Support

Packt supports all of its books with errata. While we work hard to eradicate errors from our
books, some do creep in. Many Packt books also have accompanying snippets of code to
download.

You can find errata and code downloads at `www.PacktPub.com/support`

PacktLib.PacktPub.com

PacktLib offers instant solutions to your IT questions. It is Packt's fully searchable online digital book library, accessible from any device with a web browser.

- ▸ Contains every Packt book ever published. That's over 100,000 pages of content.
- ▸ Fully searchable. Find an immediate solution to your problem.
- ▸ Copy, paste, print, and bookmark content.
- ▸ Available on demand via your web browser.

If you have a Packt account, you might want to have a look at the nine free books which you can access now on PacktLib. Head to `PacktLib.PacktPub.com` and log in or register.

Table of Contents

Preface

The incredible growth rates for the iPhone, iPod touch, and iPad have pushed consumers to a new "App" economy, with developers racing to the platform. Mobile touch-centric interfaces vary greatly from traditional computing platforms, and programmers as well as designers must learn to adapt to the new form-factor.

The iPhone User Interface Cookbook offers a complete breakdown of standard interface design on the iPhone, iPod touch, and iPad. You will learn the tools behind the trade, how to properly utilize standard interface elements, and custom UI tricks that will help your work stand out on the *App* Store.

The book is designed to be a complete overview of interface design on all iOS platforms, offering insight and an inside look into app design. A variety of topics are covered, starting with an overview of tools for the app interface designer, touching upon popular interface components such as the Tab Bar, and offering suggestions for complex game interfaces. Whether you're new to the platform or a seasoned developer with numerous applications in the App Store, this book strives to teach everyone simple and easy to implement tips for iOS interface design. Regardless of skill level, the iPhone User Interface Cookbook offers a detailed breakdown of all things interface design.

What this book covers

In the *Preface*, we'll touch upon the basic features of iOS and the common tools that we'll use as interface designers. If you're uncomfortable with the thought of being considered a designer, start your reading here.

For *Chapter 1, Getting Started: Prototyping, Proper Tools, and Testing our Design*, we'll touch upon the first steps of interface development. We'll start out with early design sketches, then progress on to the point where we put our app onto a device or offer a test build for beta users.

In *Chapter 2, Customizing our Icon, the Navigation Bar, and the Tab Bar*, we'll tackle the first thing the user sees when using our app: the icon. This 512 pixel square will be an essential piece of the puzzle if we want to see success, and we'll discuss some ways in which our work can stand out from the crowd.

Chapter 3, Different Ways To "View" our Application, is all about the different content presentation views that are available for our application. We'll discuss web views, Twitter views, modal views, and much more.

What's the difference between a Tab Bar and a Navigation View? In *Chapter 4, Utilizing Common UI Elements*, we'll tackle the various navigational interface elements that exist for our use in iOS.

Chapter 5, All About Games is action packed, as we tackle interface challenges that exist for games on iOS. Unsure about how to best go about game play mechanics or a heads up display when working with a touch platform? These recipes will help you gain a high score in interface design.

First impressions and final goodbyes are the topics that we'll take on in *Chapter 6, Starting, Stopping, and Multitasking*. From the Default.PNG to multitasking in iOS 4 and 5, we'll learn about the best ways to design our application for the stop and go nature of iOS.

Chapter 7, Notifications, Locations, and Sounds helps teach interface principles requirements that come into play when we design to include push notifications, badges, iCloud, location services, or iAds into our app. These are all common app features, and our app will be more successful if we use each correctly in our interface.

We'll discuss app configurations, copy and paste, and accessibility in *Chapter 8, Accessibility, Options, and Limited Opportunity to Help our User*. While often overlooked, the features discussed in these recipes are often responsible for the extra polish that pushes an app into the top sales charts.

Finally, for *Chapter 9, Migrating to the iPad*, we'll grow up a bit and talk about the iPad. Interface design for the larger screen and wider aspect ratio can be a bit different than the work we produce for the iPhone, and we'll discuss those differences here.

Looking for a bit more help? We'll tackle the problem of direct manipulation and the importance of application responsiveness in *Appendix A, The Importance of Direct Manipulation*.

As a final encore, we'll discuss the interface challenges that arise when designing a touch based operating system in *Appendix B, If you need a stylus, you blew it*. Software designed around use with a finger instead of a mouse can be a bit tricky, but we'll help you master the subject.

Who this book is for

The iPhone Interface Cookbook is written from the ground up for people who are new to iOS or application interface design in general. Each chapter discusses the reasoning and design strategy behind critical interface components, as well as how to best integrate each into any iPhone or iPad application. Detailed and straight-forward recipes help give guidance and build understanding far beyond what is offered through Apple's Human Interface Guidelines.

Getting to know the features of iOS

If we want to develop an attractive yet functional user interface, we need to start by taking the time to fully understand the uniqueness of the iOS operating system and how it is designed to provide an exceptional touch-centric experience. Let's take a look at the key hardware features that the user will use to interact with and experience our application.

Looking at the features...

Take note of the hardware features present on the iPhone or iPad. All iOS devices have a circle home button located below the touch-sensitive screen, volume controls found on the side of the device, a headphone jack, and a sleep button on the top of the device. On the iPhone and iPad, a switch can be found that toggles silent mode on and off.

Several other features can be found on each device, depending on the model. A **rear-facing** camera has been prevalent on the iPhone since the first model in 2007. A **front-facing camera** has become a common addition since the introduction of the iPhone 4 and **Facetime** in 2010. Recent iPod touch and iPad devices have also received front and rear cameras. All devices besides the first generation iPod touch contain a **microphone** for recording audio. With the addition of the iPhone 4S, Apple included its system-wide **Siri voice dictation software**, which is available to all applications through inclusion of the standard keyboard.

An ambient light sensor and accelerometer can be found on every iOS device. Bluetooth has been a staple of every iPhone and iPad, with iPod touches receiving the feature in 2008 models and beyond. A gyroscope is a new addition to iOS devices, being introduced with the iPhone 4 in the summer of 2010.

Music, photos, and applications are all held on the device in **flash ROM storage**. The amount of storage on each device can fluctuate anywhere between 8 GB to 64 GB and is not expandable after a user has purchased the device.

Unlike other touch capable phones or tablets, iOS devices contain no programmable hardware buttons for developers or designers to work into an application. Instead, every interaction between the user and the application must be implemented through either a software interaction with the touch screen or by utilizing the accelerometer or gyroscope for user interaction.

We've just begun to scratch the surface on the functionality available to iOS designers. Here are a few more tips that we can use to best understand the basic principles of iOS user interface development.

Understanding our audience

Fully understanding the hardware specifications and limitations for the device we're looking to target is absolutely essential. The more we know about who will be using our application and what device features they have, the better we can fine tune our user interface in order to provide a great experience for the end user.

Before we ever begin to map out any interface design, we should take the time to sit and consider where and when people will be using our application.

Imagine we are looking to build an application to help bus riders in Chicago keep track of stop locations. In this app, it wouldn't make sense to use the accelerometer and have the app update the user's location when the device is shaken, because the constant stop and go nature of a bus ride could accidentally trigger an update and frustrate the user.

Dealing with download caps

Even though Apple's cap of a 2 GB file size per application is usually more than enough space for any app, it's also important to remember that many wireless carriers across the world place a limit on the size of applications that can be downloaded over the wireless data network.

When determining a target audience and use case for an application, it's important to see what app size limitations are in place for the target market.

Using our example of an application to help bus riders find detailed stop information, it would be detrimental to have our app size be above the wireless download cap placed by the carrier, because users would be unable to download the application while walking around the city looking for a bus stop.

The tools of the trade

In designing the user interface for an iOS application, we're lucky that very few tools are required during the production process. That being said, this does mean that the tools we do need are that much more important when it comes to producing a quality application.

Let's look at what hardware and software we're going to need in order to develop the best interface possible for our application.

What we'll be using...

The first thing we need to do is pick up a capable computer for design work. Since we're developing for iOS, a Macintosh is definitely preferable if not required. If we're not going to be doing any programming, it could be possible to get away with a PC that runs Adobe *Photoshop*, but this is not recommended. Without a Macintosh, we will not have access to the iOS Simulator and other tools that Apple provides for design.

All other things being equal, a quality monitor of significant size may be the most important attribute when picking up a computer for design work. The iMac or a Mac Pro with Cinema Display may be the best option, but a Macbook or Macbook Pro is certainly sufficient. Given the Retina display of the iPhone or large display of the iPad, we'll want to have as much room for high-resolution art on our monitor as possible.

Currently, the Mac Pro is the only Apple computer that is easily upgradable after initial purchase. With a slight bit of tinkering, it's easy to add more RAM or install a new hard drive on the professional grade machine, so it should be our first choice if we're looking for a device to build upon in the future.

In comparison, it is relatively difficult to upgrade an iMac, Mac Mini, Macbook Pro, Macbook, or Macbook Air. Any Apple computer should be more than capable of producing exceptional UI design, but this lack of expandability should be something to keep in mind in case we plan on upgrading our machine down the road.

Pick up a copy of *Adobe Photoshop* and if possible, *Adobe Illustrator*. Adobe offers a variety of packages on software, which can all vary greatly in price depending on our needs and circumstances. When it comes to design and graphic production, Adobe is the gold standard and we can never go wrong by having their design suite on hand. Ultimately, *Photoshop* is really the only application we will need, but it never hurts to have Adobe's entire design suite just in case.

Many designers like working in *Illustrator* because it makes it easy to do vector drawings, which are resolution independent and work well if we ever need art for a magazine ad or promotional banner. We also never know when Apple will increase the resolution on iOS devices, as they did in 2010 with the **Retina Display**, and it is much easier to upscale artwork for higher resolution screens when resource files are easily available in vector format.

If Photoshop is out of our price range, fear not, as there are several other raster graphic programs that can help in the design process. *Acorn* by Flying Meat Software, found online at `http://flyingmeat.com/acorn/`, is an extremely capable image editor that can be purchased for only $50. *Acorn* is fundamentally similar to *Photoshop,* so moving between the two is quite easy.

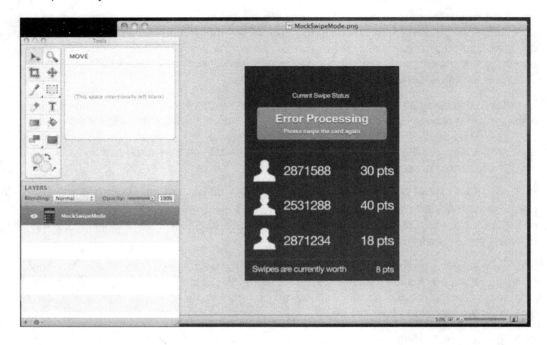

We'll also want to make sure that we've downloaded the latest version of Apple's iOS SDK tools as well. The iOS SDK can be downloaded for free from Apple's Developer Center, regardless of whether we are registered in the iOS developer program or not. When we're ready to download the SDK, we can visit `http://developer.apple.com/devcenter/ios/index.action`.

If we're not performing any of the programming for our application, we could get away without using or learning how to use the iOS SDK, but this is not preferable. The iOS SDK, along with *XCode*, allows us to change art resource files quickly and then launch the iOS Simulator to see how resources look when running in our application.

While this seems like a fairly limited tool set, we should be able to compete with nearly any user interface in the *App Store* once we have these items. Anything we can't build in code can be produced in *Photoshop*, which gives us the flexibility of only needing one application for the majority of our work. The negative side to this is that we're going to be spending a lot of time in one application, so we need to be comfortable in the image manipulation program.

We won't dive too deep into *Photoshop* in this book, so you may find yourself struggling a bit at first if you've never used the application. Luckily, there are many resources available to help teach *Photoshop*, written by individuals who are extremely talented with the application. A simple web search of the *Photoshop* technique you're looking to learn or a stop by a bookstore should provide more than enough information on improving our *Photoshop* skills.

Resources for designing iOS apps

Many websites and blogs focus primarily on the design of iOS applications. Here are a few handy resources that can help inspire and educate.

Sizing up interface elements

iDev101 offers a great breakdown of the exact sizing requirements of different iOS UI elements, which can be found at `http://www.idev101.com/code/User_Interface/sizes.html`.

The complete package

The iPhone GUI PSD `http://www.teehanlax.com/blog/2010/08/12/iphone-4-gui-psd-retina-display/` is an extremely handy Photoshop file compiled by Teehan+Lax. The file typically sees an update whenever Apple makes changes to UI elements, making this an extremely valuable resource for any designer.

Great examples from the pros

365PSD is an extremely useful site by Dutch designer Jonno Riekwel, which releases a new Photoshop file per day as a free resource. A good deal of the posts focus on iOS and the files can be a great way to learn first hand how a specific UI effect was performed in *Photoshop*. To download files from 365PSD, we should visit `http://365psd.com/`.

Working with a finger as a pointing device

In developing an operating system without a keyboard or physical buttons, Apple had to decide on whether or not to facilitate interaction with a stylus. Ultimately, it was decided that a stylus would create an unsatisfactory experience and the device was built from the ground up to only support human finger interaction.

There are many benefits in developing a touch only operating system. Users have no stylus to lose, the barrier between person and device is essentially torn down through direct interaction, and the device can easily be managed with only a thumb when held in the palm of a hand.

While often considered to be an afterthought, it's important to understand how our users will hold the device with using our application. Difference in aspect ratio, hand placement, and grip are rather serious attributes that can greatly change the development of our interface.

Let's take a look at how hands are both a blessing and a curse.

Working with our hands...

While nearly everyone who first uses an iOS device has had an experience with a traditional button based cell phone, the large screen touch based devices offer a significant difference by allowing a truly orientation independent device.

In many respects, the decision to create a device which functions as properly right side up as it does upside down was intentional on Apple's part. All iOS devices contain a single, circular, and orientation neutral button that sends the user back to the home screen upon impression. All other menus and buttons to control an application are produced on screen and as such, defined by the developer.

This establishes an incredible sense of free reign for creative design in application perspective. Games such as *Doodle Jump* by Lima Sky can offer entertaining and fast paced play mechanics while various Twitter applications can offer landscape views for reading or typing away at tweets. Applications such as *Ocarina* by Smule can flip an iPhone or iPod touch completely on its head and require a user to rotate the device completely around so that the microphone can be used to mimic an actual ocarina.

In deciding which orientation best fits our iPhone or iPod touch application, the general purpose of our app will help guide our way. In nearly every situation, the user expects the application to function properly within the portrait orientation. Unless our app is a game that requires a simulated control pad and buttons or landscape orientation, we should always assume that users will expect portrait orientation in some respect or another. Landscape can offer an intriguing and greatly appreciated bonus for many users, especially in applications that depend heavily on typing or data entry, as many users prefer typing on the larger landscape keyboard.

While the above flexibility applies to smaller iOS devices, Apple demands orientation independence when working with the iPad. Unless there is a specific reason as to why an iPad app could not support both landscape and portrait view, we're expected to design our application to fit both perspectives.

Designing visually appealing work for both portrait and landscape perspectives on the iPad can be a challenging experience. The device features a 4:3 aspect ratio which creates a screen size that's not quite a square, but not wide enough to be a true widescreen perspective either. This provides an interesting problem where it is difficult to create two unique orientation interfaces that work well in their own way.

To help account for both orientations, Apple has developed a fair amount of new interface elements for our use in an application. **Popovers** and **Dual pane views** are just two new tools that are at our disposal to help produce quality interfaces. **Tab Bar** and **Navigation Bar** views have also been redeveloped to help better fit the larger screen as well. In designing our application, we should provide some sort of dual interface perspective that best works to provide clear navigation regardless of orientation.

Instapaper - © 2008-2011 Marco Arment

Instapaper by Marco Arment implements a prime example of an iPad application that provides a dual pane interface when in landscape view and a single pane presentation aided by a Popover sheet when in portrait view.

When holding an iPhone in portrait view, the thumb of the hand holding device is easily available for use on screen. This portrait view also allows for the opposite hand to also be used as a way to interact with the device with ease. When holding an iPhone in landscape view, the device is typically held in a fashion that allows for only the thumb of each hand to be used to interact with the screen. As such, the landscape perspective is best used for typing or game applications.

Due to the large size of the iPad, the device offers a different experience with regards to holding and interacting with the screen. Typically, the iPad is held with two hands much like a book, with one hand lifting up to touch on screen with the pointer finger when input is needed. A large bezel surrounding the device prevents a finger from accidentally coming in contact with screen and makes it difficult for a thumb to move from a relaxed position to the screen. This distance makes applications or games with persistent interaction, such as a game with a software simulated control stick, difficult to play for extended periods of time because the hand will naturally fatigue while being held up to touch the screen.

With this information in mind, we should be able to develop applications that behave predictably for the user. When the user knows what to expect with our app, time spent learning the application will diminish and users will have more time to enjoy our work.

Screen sizes and the touch surface can vary based on the device, which means we shouldn't assume a great iPhone app will automatically make a successful iPad app.

It all depends on how you hold it

While the iPad and iPhone both run iOS, the size difference between the two devices can cause us to hold each considerably different. The iPhone and iPod touch are primarily one-hand devices while the iPad is more commonly held with two hands like a book.

Just because an interface works well on an iPhone doesn't mean it will necessarily translate to the bigger device and vice versa. Likewise, actions that work well with in one way on iPhone may need a different gesture or a button on iPad.

These size differences help demonstrate why we should have multiple test devices on hand during development. Just because one mechanic works well on a specific device doesn't mean we should assume that it would work well on another.

Placing visual elements for touch

Being devoid of physical buttons, there are a few assumptions that we can make about our user base and how they'll interact with our app. Because nearly any interface imaginable is possible on the touch screen, it's important that we abide by documents like **Apple's Human Interface Guidelines**, which are written with perspective from designers who had a hand in the creation of the platform's interface elements.

Apple's *Human Interface Guidelines* are exhaustive documents published on the iOS and Mac Dev Centers, located at `http://developer.apple.com`, for developers to learn how Apple intends interface items to be used inside applications.

Determining placement of standard components...

In designing placement of components of our app interface, we should first understand what is required of us and should be placed in a specific location without compromise in all situations. Apple has established their Human Interface Guidelines, which detail procedures and specifications that must be followed by all applications and our work could get rejected by their review team if we decide to disobey these recommendations.

The most important thing to keep in mind with touch is that we should follow Apple's recommendations on placement of common UI elements. Essential elements such as the **Navigation Bar** and **Tab Bar** are placed on the top and bottom of the screen respectively for a reason. The high placement of the Navigation Bar serves the purpose of giving title and context to the information that is directly below, allowing us to move throughout an expansive table of information easily, much like thumbing through a stack of papers on a desk would be much simpler if the top of each page had an accurate title.

The Navigation Bar's placement anchored to the bottom of the screen allows for easy movement throughout multiple modal views without ever obstructing important information on screen with our finger. With just a quick touch, we can quickly swap between two or three important pages of data.

Not to be confused with a misplacement of the Navigation Bar in the Tab Bar location, many apps such as *Maps* or *Calendar* place a **Toolbar** anchored to the bottom of the screen that looks nearly identical to the Navigation Bar. As shown in the next screenshot, the two look similar but serve different purposes:

Calendar - © 2007-2011 Apple Inc.

The Navigation Bar allows the user to navigate through vast tables of information either forward or backwards quickly. Anchoring a similar Toolbar to the bottom of the screen for various settings, as we find in *Safari*, allows for users to quickly manipulate data on screen with clear buttons. We should be sure to follow these established conventions with regards to navigation.

Action sheets can often be implemented in an app upon pressing an item in the Toolbar. Action sheets offer quick and temporary choice between several different options. For an example of an action sheet, open *Safari* and tap the plus icon located in the center of the bottom Toolbar. As shown in the next screenshot, this option brings up three temporary choices that can be quickly chosen by the user:

Keyboard placement anchored to the bottom of the screen is also a necessity for interface development. Whereas the software keys are not physically responsive to the press like the keyboard on our Mac or PC, the placement of each button becomes a trained response much like a tactile device. Custom keyboards in general can be a detrimental decision for our application in nearly every situation. Their sizing will confuse our users and be unnatural in comparison to every other keyboard on the device, leading to an unnecessary learning curve that causes frustration.

Picker views for date or different selection options are sized to fit into the same size of the Keyboard and should mimic placement conventions of the Keyboard as well. Whenever we implement this option, it should be anchored to the bottom of the screen and only be displayed when necessary.

Clock - © 2007-2011 Apple Inc.

As demonstrated about with the Clock application's alarm feature, Picker Views are expected to be anchored to the bottom of the screen and we should follow this guideline when implementing the control in our applications.

With regards to placing significant text and data on screen for our user, we should create conventional typography that preferably aligns flush left, at a size that is easily legible to the user. In creating labels or bodies of text, we'll often be using code similar to this:

```
cell.textLabel.font = [UIFontfontWithName:@"HelveticaNeue-Bold"
size:17];
```

Correct text size is a subjective metric depending upon our audience and typeface, so it may often be helpful to provide multiple sizing options to our users when possible. If using a common font like Helvetica, we should try to make our text size 16 or larger if we want our work to be easily legible.

[For an example of well-placed text, we should follow the example of *Notes* and *Mail* with placement of either user entered or pre-defined text.]

If we feel unsure about proper placement of a specific user interface element on screen, it is best to follow Apple's lead on whatever we're doing. Using Apple developed applications that come pre-installed on our iOS device is the best way to experience quality examples of how interface elements should be properly placed.

There's more...

If we're looking to create a mobile webpage for our business or personal website, there are several basic web principles that we should be cautious of during our development. Here are a few tips for producing exceptional mobile HTML.

Comments on columns

Multicolumn blocks of text are a web staple, with significant prevalence on many blogs and news sites. However, columns work poorly on the iPhone or iPod touch, as constant scrolling both vertically and horizontally can become confusing. We should refrain from using such a scheme and instead create a single column, even if it must be rather lengthy.

It all depends on how you hold it

When designing for a desktop computer application or website, it's natural to place important navigation or action items near the top, bottom, or corners of the screen.

Placement of interface elements near sides of the screen is an extremely effective design principle on the desktop because of an interaction model called **Fitts's Law**.

In the simplest explanation, we place interface elements near the corner of the screen when working with a mouse because when the user moves the cursor from the center of the screen to a button near an edge, it's more difficult to miss the target because the cursor stops when it hits the screen boundary and as such, buttons placed there effectively have infinite widths.

While Fitts's Law works wonderfully with a mouse, it's less important and can create cramped interfaces when practiced on iOS. Since our user will be using their fingers, which are typically slower pointing devices which give the brain more time to adjust for distance in movement and in turn provides for greater accuracy, it's alright to utilize space in the center of the screen and space buttons further apart.

What you need for this book

To tackle the recipes inside of this book, you'll be best served to have the following equipment on hand: a Macintosh computer running *Snow Leopard* or *Lion* operating systems, an iPhone, iPod touch, or iPad device, a copy of Adobe's *Photoshop* software, and sketching tools such as a notepad and pencil. Throughout the book, we will refer to additional software and tools that can help make interface creation easier; however these side notes will never be required during the design process.

Conventions

In this book, you will find a number of styles of text that distinguish between different kinds of information. Here are some examples of these styles, and an explanation of their meaning.

Code words in text are shown as follows: "We can include other contexts through the use of the `include` directive."

A block of code is set as follows:

```
<rdf:Description rdf:about=""
        xmlns:dc="http://purl.org/dc/elements/1.1/">
    <dc:format>application/vnd.adobe.photoshop</dc:format>
</rdf:Description>
```

When we wish to draw your attention to a particular part of a code block, the relevant lines or items are set in bold:

```
<rdf:Description rdf:about=""
        xmlns:dc="http://purl.org/dc/elements/1.1/">
    <dc:format>application/vnd.adobe.photoshop</dc:format>
</rdf:Description>
```

Any command-line input or output is written as follows:

```
# cp /usr/src/asterisk-addons/configs/cdr_mysql.conf.sample
```

New terms and **important words** are shown in bold. Words that you see on the screen, in menus or dialog boxes for example, appear in the text like this: "clicking the **Next** button moves you to the next screen".

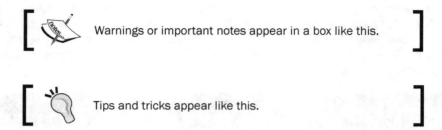

Warnings or important notes appear in a box like this.

Tips and tricks appear like this.

Reader feedback

Feedback from our readers is always welcome. Let us know what you think about this book—what you liked or may have disliked. Reader feedback is important for us to develop titles that you really get the most out of.

To send us general feedback, simply send an e-mail to feedback@packtpub.com, and mention the book title via the subject of your message.

If there is a book that you need and would like to see us publish, please send us a note in the **SUGGEST A TITLE** form on www.packtpub.com or e-mail suggest@packtpub.com.

If there is a topic that you have expertise in and you are interested in either writing or contributing to a book, see our author guide on www.packtpub.com/authors.

Customer support

Now that you are the proud owner of a Packt book, we have a number of things to help you to get the most from your purchase.

Downloading the example code

You can download the example code files for all Packt books you have purchased from your account at http://www.PacktPub.com. If you purchased this book elsewhere, you can visit http://www.PacktPub.com/support and register to have the files e-mailed directly to you.

Errata

Although we have taken every care to ensure the accuracy of our content, mistakes do happen. If you find a mistake in one of our books—maybe a mistake in the text or the code—we would be grateful if you would report this to us. By doing so, you can save other readers from frustration and help us improve subsequent versions of this book. If you find any errata, please report them by visiting http://www.packtpub.com/support, selecting your book, clicking on the **errata submission form** link, and entering the details of your errata. Once your errata are verified, your submission will be accepted and the errata will be uploaded on our website, or added to any list of existing errata, under the Errata section of that title. Any existing errata can be viewed by selecting your title from http://www.packtpub.com/support.

Piracy

Piracy of copyright material on the Internet is an ongoing problem across all media. At Packt, we take the protection of our copyright and licenses very seriously. If you come across any illegal copies of our works, in any form, on the Internet, please provide us with the location address or website name immediately so that we can pursue a remedy.

Please contact us at copyright@packtpub.com with a link to the suspected pirated material.

We appreciate your help in protecting our authors, and our ability to bring you valuable content.

Questions

You can contact us at questions@packtpub.com if you are having a problem with any aspect of the book, and we will do our best to address it.

1

Getting Started: Prototyping, Proper Tools, and Testing our Design

In this chapter, we will cover:

- ► Starting with the sketch
- ► Developing a rapid prototype
- ► Migrating to the high-resolution Retina display
- ► Getting our app onto a device
- ► When to use the simulator or a real device
- ► User testing and getting a way for people to test out our app
- ► Taking a screenshot of an application on our device
- ► Working within Apple's guidelines

Introduction

As an introduction to interface design and development on the iPhone, it's important to learn about the basic skills that we'll need to be comfortable with in order to tackle our first design project.

We'll dive into more technical topics later on, but first we'll start by discussing the different tools of the trade, hardware features that we'll need to focus our design around, and placing our design work on an actual device.

In this chapter, we'll tackle these introductory lessons and gain a foundation for what it will take to jump into the world of iPhone and iPad application user interface design.

Starting with the sketch

Before we take time to design our user interface in Photoshop, it is important to sit down with a piece of paper and a pencil to sketch out the basics for how users will interact with our app. Once we set a programmer out to begin work on an application with a given interface, it can be very costly to go back and make changes later when we realize that our design has a few small problems that need to be fixed.

Luckily, a notebook and pencil are cheap tools, and we can draw out many example interfaces without ever wasting a dollar of programming time.

Getting ready

For best results, we should find a desk, a good pencil, an eraser, and a couple of pieces of paper. If available, large notepads are preferable, as the extra space will allow room for notes.

How to do it...

Before we step into **Adobe Photoshop** or **XCode** with our application design, we should begin by sketching out the idea onto paper.

 Photoshop is Adobe's high-profile raster image editing software. XCode is Apple's development environment for iOS and Mac applications. Both apps are essential parts of our development toolbox.

Let's take a look at some basic iOS drawing principles so that we can best prepare our sketches for the transition to pixels on an iPhone screen:

1. We should start by sketching several rough boxes that are scaled roughly to the size of an iPhone or iPad. The iPhone screen is a rectangle measuring approximately 4.5 inches by 2.5 inches. The iPad screen measures approximately 9 inches by 7 inches.

   Next, we should go about designing a wire frame mock up of how we anticipate interacting with our application, so that we know exactly what we are looking for in our prototype. The following screenshot shows how a wire frame should give a visual representation of how the user will flow through the final application. In the quick wire frame of a dictionary application below, we gain a good idea as to how the user will interact with our work.

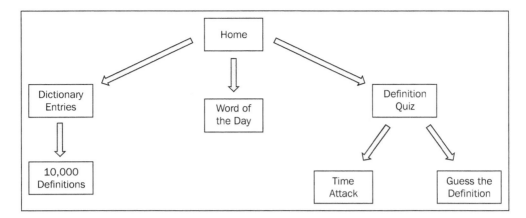

2. The paper is literally our blank canvas right now, so we should experiment with ideas and get an idea of what we want our app to look like.

    Often, it's useful if large sketch paper is used when designing an interface. This allows space for notes and multiple screens to be sketched.

    We'll be designing an application in either landscape or portrait view, and may want to place out multiple possible screens on our page of sketch paper to help lay out an intended application flow.

    From here, we can begin to sketch out our interface on screen. Buttons, text, and other interface elements can be placed in the approximate size and position that we desire our future app to look like.

3. With our application screens laid out on paper, you begin to literally place the paper in your hand and touch it as if it were a real iOS device.

    Take a quick note of the visual changes that occur when a finger is placed upon the interface. Does touching a button cause the user to place their hand over important data? Do buttons seem to be spaced far enough apart that a user could easily tap on one without errantly tapping upon another?

4. Take notes on the process of interacting with your sketched mock up application and proceed to make changes to the sketch, and then repeat the process.

    Ideally, we will go through three or four revisions until we design something that we could see ourselves enjoying on our iOS device.

5. At this point, our drawings may be slightly sporadic and our notes may be messy. Since the reasoning behind our design is still fresh in our minds, now would be the best time to go back and redraw views or notes that are unclear. Once we're happy with our work, we are done sketching up our application.

How it works...

Because iOS devices require a user to physically interact with a variety of interface elements in a small amount of space, sketching up ideas can be a powerful way to test user interface design ideas. If drawn close to scale, we can simulate touch interactions and get a good idea of how our interface will look before we ever paint a pixel in *Photoshop*.

There's more...

Several companies provide special graph paper, stencils, and iOS applications that help make it easier to sketch application ideas. Typically these products are inexpensive and make high quality mock ups simple. Many stencil sets also come with many standard UI elements accurately sized, which will allow us to sketch with confidence and precision.

Picking up the best stencil set

Design Commission produces arguably the best interface design stencils, which can be found at `http://www.uistencils.com/products/iphone-stencil-kit`. For a low cost, iPhone and iPad stencils can be purchased along with appropriate device sketchpads. Design Commission also has great stencil sets for Android and Web developers, in case we're looking to design for those platforms as well.

As we can see in the following screenshot, the interface stencil contains many common pieces and can help in properly laying out elements on paper:

There's an app for that

There are even several iOS applications focused around making the sketching process easier as well. *Interface* by Less Code LTD, *iMockups for iPad* by Endloop Systems, and *Dapp* by Kerofrog are all great applications that can make the mock up process easier. Each offers the ability to drag and drop standard interface elements around on a real iPhone or iPod touch screen, allowing us to quickly grasp the scale and feel of our desired interface on a real device.

See also

▸ *Developing a rapid prototype in this chapter*

▸ *Getting our work onto a device in this chapter*

Developing a rapid prototype

Sketching up an application design is a critical step in designing an exceptional user experience, but it doesn't quite compare to actually using our fingers to interact with our interface on a real iOS device.

No matter how well we sketch up our interface, we may come upon a problem wherein a certain aspect of our design doesn't really work well once it's implemented on an iOS device. Sometimes, these design problems are minor and altering our interface to fix the problem isn't a big deal. But there is also the real possibility that a design mistake can be a showstopper, requiring hours of new design work and programming for something that could have been easily solved before development began.

Getting ready

When preparing to put together a rapid prototype, we should first consult with our programmer. There are several different ways to go about developing a rapid prototype, with each having different pros and cons.

Arguably the best way to create a rapid prototype is to literally develop the shell of the application using Apple's suite of development tools for Macintosh and iPhone applications, *XCode*. This will allow the app to run natively on our test device and also create code that can be used in the final application.

However, there may be situations where developing a rapid prototype in *XCode* would actually be extremely time intensive and not worth the effort. In these scenarios, there are several other ways to build a simple rapid prototype, which we will discuss in this recipe.

How to do it...

Rapid prototypes can be an exceptional asset to the standard development cycle, allowing us to gain an idea of how our application will work before we spend a good deal of costly time on development. Here are the steps that will help us prepare a rapid prototype:

1. Much like we did in the previous recipe, we should begin by constructing a wireframe of our application.

    This will help us to get an idea as to how our application will flow and what screens will be required for our work.

2. Next, we should go about sketching out each of our intended screens so that we have an expected design for our rapid prototype.

    We don't need to add an exceptional amount of polish or have our design be 100 percent completed, but it will be useful to have an idea as to what we're planning for the application to look like.

3. After we have a wire frame to visualize application flow, we should go about determining how to build the prototype application with the least amount of content possible.

    For example, if we're building a dictionary application, what would be the fewest number of entries we need in order to make sure that our design and concept works? As a rule of thumb, we should have enough substance in our prototype to not have doubts about the success of any feature in the application.

4. With our prototype planned, we should go forward with programming our basic application in whatever format that works the best.

    If we have the time, it's often best to produce an actual app in *XCode* for our rapid prototype, as this will give us a significant code base to start with when we begin work on the final application. However, this method is often time consuming and costly, so we may decide to go by another route.

 Several iOS applications have been produced to aid in the development of rapid prototypes. The best example of an iOS native prototyping tool is the simple *Prototypes* app for Mac by Duncan Wilcox, which can be found on the Mac App Store. Prototypes relies upon its own basic programming language in order to connect different pages of our prototype together, but is a powerful tool for the development of quick prototypes that will run on a real iOS device without requiring XCode.

As seen below, With *Prototypes*, mock screenshots are given simple properties that are used to contain different attributes of our rapid prototype:

Prototypes - © iridescent.co

5. If we are looking to avoid XCode and Prototypes, we can design our prototype in basic **HTML** instead.

   Several open source HTML and **JavaScript** frameworks exist for web developers looking to build a mobile friendly website and these tools can be used for prototyping an application as well.

 jQTouch, found online at `http://jqtouch.com/`, is a great jQuery plugin that allows for rapid prototyping of web apps that can be used to test the flow of our application before we go about building our native app.

With a prototype built, we can go about testing our interface ideas for usability and simplicity. It's much easier to alter spacing and button layout on a prototype than it is in a final application and now is the time to verify that our design ideas will make sense when translated onto a physical iOS device.

How it works...

iOS designers are at a bit of a disadvantage with prototyping when compared to traditional web developers or even desktop application developers.

Interface interaction with a mouse and keyboard has been commonplace for 30 years and most designers have grown to understand basic interface concepts that either work well or fail miserably. In contrast, touch-based interface development is still in its infancy and has really only been prevalent since the launch of the iPhone in 2007.

It's still possible for iOS designers to overcome this competitive disadvantage and develop a great touch-centric interface; it just requires a bit more work. If we start each project with a quick, rapid prototype, we'll help guarantee that we're not sent back to the drawing board late in development because of failed design work.

See also

▶ *Getting your application onto a real device in this chapter*

Migrating to the high-resolution Retina display

With the announcement of the iPhone 4, Apple introduced the **Retina display**. This new technology produces a 3.5 screen with a resolution of 960x640 pixels, which is considered to be the highest resolution screen ever placed inside of a mobile phone. The screen's pixel density is a welcome addition to consumers, but can cause a significant heartache for designers who are unprepared for the change. In this recipe, we'll take a look at how to best prepare resources for future changes in iOS screen resolution.

Getting ready

Updating our art resources for the new screen requires us to double the resolution of our original artwork. To help make this process easier, we'll need the original art resources for our application. Otherwise we'll be producing new high-resolution artwork from scratch, which can be a significant obstacle to overcome.

How to do it...

Now and in the future, it's to be expected that all iPhone and iPod touch devices will feature the high resolution Retina display. If we want success for our application, we should prepare our artwork for the 326 pixel per inch screen.

Let's take a look at a few steps that will help us migrate to the larger screen:

1. We should start by going through our old applications and prepare to update outdated resources for the higher resolution display.

Luckily, Apple has built iOS to properly upscale all standard UI elements that are drawn natively in code or through **Interface Builder**. Text will also be scaled properly depending upon the device, so we don't need to worry about changing any `UITextViews` either. The only real concern will come into play with art resources, typically stored as .PNG files. Isolate these files so that we have an idea as to what needs to be updated for the Retina display.

2. Next, we hope that our original art files were created either as vectors, or as raster pieces greater in resolution than 640 pixels by 960 pixels, that were scaled down for the iPhone. If either of the previous two statements is true, we're fairly well off. If not, we've got a bit of a rough road ahead of us.

Vector and raster images

 Vector graphic files are a type of image format where visual data is stored as a geometrical set of points, lines, curves, or polygons. Vector graphics scale up well because images are displayed as shapes with a specific mathematical relationship, meaning that magnifying the image is no problem because the relationship between the shapes stays the same regardless of size. Vector graphics can be built with an application like _Adobe Illustrator_ but can be somewhat more difficult to use than _Photoshop_. If our art resources are still available in a vector format, we only need to create new copies of each resource at double the resolution of the old file. Once we do this, we're ready to move forward and prepare these new files for inclusion into our application.

Raster images are built as a grid of square pixels, with each point in the grid having a set color. It is difficult to increase the size of raster graphics because a multiplication in size just means that there will be a multiplication in the amount of pixels that build the image. As such, raster images tend to look pixilated or blurry when increased in size. Doubling the size of a raster graphic will look unprofessional and isn't likely to be of high enough quality for our application.

More likely however, we'll find that our resource files have been saved and only remain in a raster format like PNG:

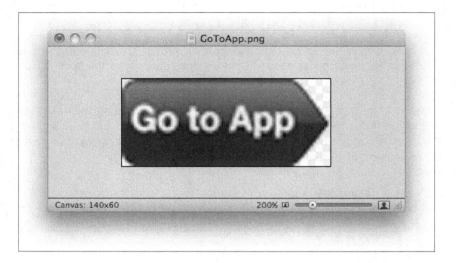

If, at this point, we're left with only raster images and have no access to either higher resolution artwork or vector images, we have a bit of a predicament on our hands. The tough reality of this situation is that we'll have to go about creating each piece of art again by hand at double its original resolution in order to fit the Retina display.

3. After we've gone about updating our resource art for the Retina display, it's time to update the file names of each piece for inclusion into our app project.

   Due to exceptional engineering by Apple's iOS team, it's extremely simple to name our high-resolution art so that our app knows how to handle these new files. To properly name our high-resolution files, we only need to append @2x onto the file name of the low-resolution resource file name.

   For example, if we have a resource called Button.PNG, we need to name our new double resolution resource file as Button@2x.PNG.

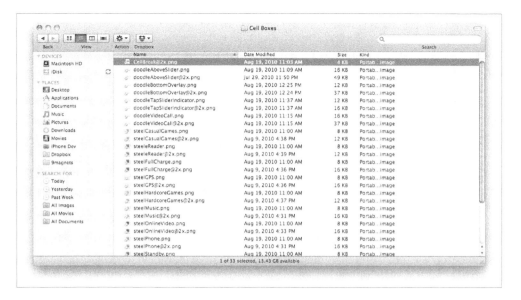

4. Once we've renamed all new high-resolution resource files to include the @2x suffix, we're ready to hand the new files off to our programmer or include them into the XCode project ourselves.

5. We should take the new files and include them into the *XCode* project as we would do to any other art file and that's it. There's no need to play around with any code or project settings; just leave the new art in the same resource folder as the original resource file.

    At this point, our application should be well prepared for the Retina display. No matter if our user has the high-resolution screen or not, our application will continue to look great.

How it works...

Apple has developed iOS and *XCode* so that inclusion of artwork for the Retina display is extremely simple. The operating system is designed to recognize if an iOS device is utilizing the Retina display, and then display the correct resource file size for the specific device. If a Retina display is detected, then the @2x art is used. If not, then the original piece of art is displayed instead.

There's more...

The introduction of the Retina display with the iPhone 4 was a wonderful example of why designers should create artwork in either a vector format or in a size much larger than they ever intend on using. While it is easy to take something big and make it smaller, it's extremely difficult to take something small and make it bigger.

Don't get too comfortable

Even though the Retina unbelievably displays high pixel density of 326 pixels per inch, it seems to be at an upper limit which Apple will likely not increase. Hence, we should prepare for the future by creating artwork at much higher resolutions that we should ever need, just in case.

Hiring someone to help fix our art problem

Since the emergence of the Retina display, several web companies have begun to specialize in the up scaling of mobile phone art for higher resolution displays. We should be wary of hiring such a company, as there are no magical techniques that can automatically increase the size of our low-resolution artwork.

If we do decide to work with a company that specializes in up scaling, we should ask for the contact information of previous clients to insure that the company completely redraws artwork for the higher resolution. We don't want to get stuck paying for artwork that was just magnified in *Photoshop*.

See also

  ▶ *Accounting for resolution and aspect ratio changes in Chapter 9*

Getting our work onto a device

Once we've planned out our interface and started working on development, we'll need to set up an iOS device for testing. By using *XCode* and Apple's iOS Dev Center, we'll be able to send pre-release application builds to our iOS device using a standard 30-pin connection cable.

Getting ready

Before we start, we'll want to gather up the iOS device we plan on using for testing, the latest update to the iOS SDK from the **iOS Dev Center**, and the computer we plan on doing our design work on.

Apple typically keeps a collection of PDFs and videos on the iOS Provisioning Portal, which are much more thorough and up-to-date than this recipe. It would be beneficial to download and read or watch these resources before we begin.

We should also complete this recipe using the **Team Agent** credentials for our iOS developer account. Apple has two different accounts that we can choose from depending upon our needs as developers. All accounts currently cost $100 per year and allow us to release an unlimited number of apps into the *App Store*. Little is needed to sign up besides the bank account information and any legal business filings that we may have if we are registering as a company instead of an individual.

Individual accounts are fairly self-explanatory, working best for people looking to release apps under their personal name. If we sign up as an individual, our account log-in serves as the Team Agent.

Company accounts are for development studios that may have two or more developers or designers who all need access to the iOS Development Center forums or operating system pre-release builds. For a company account, the log-in credentials used to create the account is the Team Agent account and this will be needed to create the necessary files for this recipe.

How to do it...

Setting up our computer to process pre-release builds is one of the most difficult tasks that we'll accomplish early on as iOS developers. It's a fairly complex job and can be very confusing at first. Here are some simple steps to help get our test application running on an iPhone, iPod touch, or iPad:

1. In preparing our application and device for testing, we're going to build what is called a **Provisioning Profile**. This file is required for applications that we want to test on a device and will include information from our **Development Certificate**, **Device UDID**, and **App ID**. The Provisioning Profile works with XCode, iTunes, and our device to make sure that we're running an authentic copy of our app.

   First, acquire the iOS Development Certificate by generating a **Certificate Signing Request** with **Keychain Access**. This process will give your applications the appropriate private key required for an iOS device to run our application.

Launch **Keychain Access** from our Applications folder in OS X. Next, visit the **Preferences** window, which can be found in the **Keychain Access** menu bar or by using the *Command + comma* keyboard shortcut. Navigate over to the **Certificates** tab, and then turn **Online Certificate Status Protocol** and **Certificate Revocation List** modes off before closing the **Preferences** window.

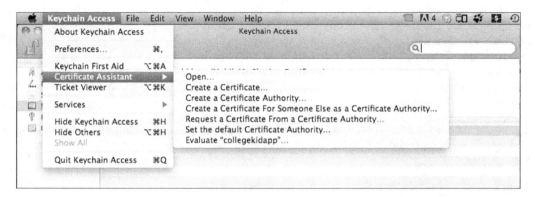

2. Next, go back to the menu bar and select **Request a Certificate from a Certificate Authority** under the **Certificate Assistant** menu item.

3. When filling out the **Certificate Assistant** form, be sure to use the email address that is associated with our iOS Team Agent Apple account.

4. Fill out the **Common Name** field, leave **CA Email Address** blank, click on the **Saved to Disk** radio button, select **Let Me Specify Key Pair**, and then click on **Continue** to proceed.

5. Select **2048 bits** key size and **RSA** algorithm options when prompted on the next screen. After clicking on **Continue**, a CSR file will be created on our computer's desktop.

6. Now log into the iOS Provisioning Portal using our Team Agent account. Click upon the **Certificates** navigation option, then click on **Request Certificate** under the **Development** tab.

7. Scroll down the page, click on **Choose File**, then select the CSR file from our desktop.

8. After successfully submitting the file, an email should be sent to the Team Admin and the status of our uploaded certificate will change to **Pending Approval**. The Team Agent account user can then approve the certificate request and a new certificate will be available for download in the **Certificates** menu in the iOS Provisioning Portal.

9. Once downloaded, double click the new `.cer` file and install the certificate using Keychain Access. This new certificate will last for a year before it expires, after which we'll have to go through this whole process again.

10. With our new certificate loaded onto our computer through **Keychain Access**, we're now ready to configure our test device through XCode. We should now tether our iOS device to our computer through the standard 30-pin connecter and launch iTunes.

    Once the device finishes the sync process, select the device under the **Devices** menu and click on the **Summary** tab. Now we'll want to use our mouse to click on the device serial number that is located near the top of the window. This will reveal our device's UDID, which we can select by using the *Command+C* copy shortcut.

iTunes - © 2001-2011 Apple Inc.

Then we head back to our web browser and the iOS Provisioning Portal, where we can select the **Devices** menu option. Click the **Add Devices** button, enter a device name, and then paste in the device UDID using the *Command+V* paste shortcut. Click on **Submit** and our device has now been configured as a test device.

11. We now need to create an App ID, which is a unique identifier that Apple uses as part of the Provisioning Profile. App IDs help make special iOS features like in **App Purchase**, **Push Notification**, or **Game Center** work.

    Using our Team Agent account, log into the iOS Provisioning Portal and navigate to the **App ID** menu section. Click the **New App ID** button and give a short description for our App ID. For the **Bundle Seed ID** drop down option, either generate a new Bundle Seed ID or use a previous ID. We would use a previously generated ID if we wanted our application to share data with an existing application.

    Now we should enter a **Bundle Identifier** into the text field. This identifier should match the CF Bundle Identifier that has been set for the app under the **Application Settings** in XCode. If we ever plan on using features like in **App Purchase** or Push Notifications in our app, we should use a unique Bundle Identifier. Apple suggests the `com.companyname.appname` format, to guarantee that our Bundle Identifier is unique across all IDs. For example, a company called ABC Software with an application called **Our Great App** would create a Bundle Identifier called `com.abcsoftware.ourgreatapp`.

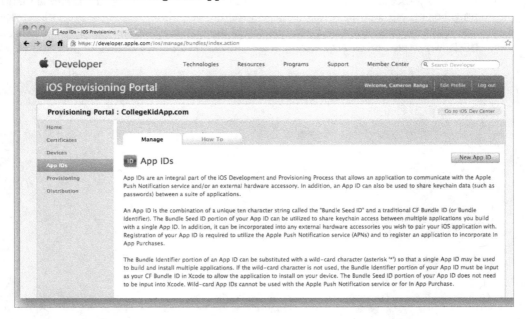

Once we click on the **Submit** button, our Bundle Seed ID will be created and connected to our new Bundle identifier and this new string is our App ID.

12. Since we've now created our development certificate, registered our test device, and created an App ID, we can move forward and create the actual Provisioning Profile for our application. Using this new profile, we can successfully send a test application to a device and finally try out our application.

    Using our Team Agent account, visit the **Provisioning** menu section of the iOS Provisiong Portal. Click on the **Add** button and give a name to our new Provisioning Profile. We should then click the check buttons for each device that we want to test our application on. Finally, we should select the Developer Certificate and unique App ID that we want to use for our application.

    After entering in all of this information, click on the **Submit** button and a new Provisioning Profile will be created which we can use to test our application. While still in the **Provisioning** section of the iOS Provisioning Portal, we can download our new profile and save it to our computer.

13. Once the Provisioning File has finished downloading, drag the file from Finder to XCode or iTunes to install the profile. We should now launch XCode and open the **Organizer** under the **Window** menu bar option. As long as our iOS device is still connected, we should see it here in the side menu. Under the provisioning option in the window, click the plus button and locate the Provisioning Profile if it isn't already selected.

14. At this point, we've successfully created a provisioning profile for our test application. Now head to our project file in XCode, select the project from the **Target** option in the side bar, then hit the blue **Info** button up on the toolbar. Scroll down and set the **Code Signing Identity** field to developer certificate associated with our new Provisioning Profile. We can now close the **Info** window.

We can now run our application in *XCode*. We can now use any iOS device to test with, however it is often wise not to use a device that you depend on daily for testing. While there are few repercussions with regards to using a device for testing, it's better to be safe than sorry with a device that you need as a phone or for other work related items.

 To test out our app, we can click on the **Build and Go** menu bar option in order to build the app on our tethered iOS device.

How it works...

Installing an application on a test device can be a bit lengthy the first time we go through the process but will become much easier for sequential applications, as we no longer will need to create a developer certificate or register our test device.

Apple's designed the system to make sure that we can securely install pre-release software on devices without fear of our work being pirated or reverse engineered by those looking to take our ideas. The profile system also helps protect users from nefarious developers who may otherwise look to deliver malware applications by circumventing the App Store.

The certificates, profiles, and application IDs that we create will be specific to our developer account, our applications, and our test devices. So unless we specifically intend to run a test application on a specific device, no unintended eyes will be able to see our pre-release work.

Once we've set up our application's Provisioning Profile, we'll be able to run our application as much as we would like on our test device. The benefits of testing our app on a real iOS device will become immediately apparent and we'll forget all about the heartache we went through to get our application up and running in the first place.

There's more...

Two iOS devices are better than one, and we may find ourselves in a situation where we would like to add multiple iOS devices to our developer account through the Provisioning Portal at one time. Luckily, Apple has developed a method for simplifying this process:

Setting up multiple devices at once

If we're looking to set up multiple iOS test devices at the same time, we can bulk upload the device names and UDIDs using the *iPhone Configuration Utility* or by creating a tab delimited `.txt` file. Once we've created a file containing all of our device information, we can upload it through the iOS Developer Portal by clicking on the **Upload Devices** button under the **Devices** menu option.

How many devices should we use?

We've discussed setting up test devices, but how many different devices should we use? Should we test on both the iPhone and the iPad?

Ideally, we'll test on as many devices as we can afford. However, we should test on a minimum of three devices. The first should be an iPhone or iPod touch running the latest operating system version available. The second should be an older iPhone or iPod touch running the oldest operating system that we plan on supporting. Finally, we should also test on an iPad, even if we haven't optimized for the tablet interface.

See also

▶ *Tools of the trade in the Preface*

Taking a screenshot of an application on our device

In designing our interface for an application, we're going to be working with pre-release builds where our interface and app features will be changing quite often. We'll find ourselves working on an interface, throwing images or new text into an app to test, and then we'll probably make a few more changes and repeat this process.

It will be useful to take screenshots of our work in progress to email over for viewing on a larger monitor or to send to a friend or project teammate.

In this recipe, we'll learn how to quickly take and email screenshots of an application.

Getting ready

For this application, we'll only need our iOS device. We may also want the charging and syncing connection cable that game with our device to sync images with a computer if this is desirable.

How to do it...

It doesn't matter if we're using an iPhone, iPod touch, or iPad, as the process for taking a screenshot is the same on all devices. Let's take a look at the simple process:

1. We should start by loading the application and specific view that we desire to take a screenshot of on our iOS device.

    Start by heading to the application that we want to take a screenshot of, and keep it open on our iOS device.

2. Next, we should hold down on the sleep button sitting on the top right or left of the device and then quickly press down the home button.

    Both buttons must be pressed at the same time for the screenshot to be taken. It may take a bit of practice to not put the device to sleep while taking a screenshot.

3. We should see a white flash, indicating that a screenshot was successfully taken. Next, we need to go into the *Photos* application.

    Once we see the white flash of light on screen, we'll know that the screenshot had been taken successfully and we can move on to the *Photos* app to send the screenshot to our email inbox.

4. Our screenshot will show up as the last taken photo, so we can now email, print, MMS, or upload the photo to a computer using *iPhoto*.

In *Photos*, we can send or upload the image however we see fit and then use this screenshot to help improve our interface further.

How it works...

Apple has designed a simple, intuitive way to take a screenshot of any screen in iOS. The problem is, there is little obvious instruction on how to actually perform this function and most users are unaware that the feature even exists.

But once we're able to take screenshots, we'll find ourselves often taking quick screens as a way to quickly get our work in progress from the iPhone onto a traditional computer for further inspection.

See also

▶ *Getting our work onto a device in this chapter*

Working within Apple's guidelines

The guidelines placed upon developers by Apple have been a hot topic of debate since the *App Store* first opened in 2007. For over two years, applications were rejected from the store with a vague explanation as to what was or was not acceptable for sale within Apple's walled garden.

Luckily, Apple has been much more open in recent history with regards to what is allowed in the *App Store*. Many common reasons for rejection involve problems with an app's user interface, so it is important for designers to understand why rules are in place so that a costly app rejection can be avoided.

Getting ready

Apple provides two important documents to help designers keep applications from being rejected. We should take the time to download and study these documents before sending off our application to Apple. The first document is called the **iPhone User Interface Guidelines**, and this file can be found in its most up to date version on the iOS Dev Center. This detailed document offers a bit of detail and reasoning as to why it is important that iOS interface elements should behave correctly in every application.

Next, we should become familiar with the *App Store Review Guidelines* document that can also be found in the iOS Dev Center portal. These guidelines were first published in September 2010 as a way to offer explanation of the rules and regulations for approval into the *App* Store reviewers.

Once we've read both of these documents, we're ready to start glancing over our application user interface to make sure that we abide by all *App Store* regulations.

How to do it...

Keeping within Apple's requirements isn't difficult so long as we keep focused on the requirements and prepare accordingly. Here are a few steps to help keep our app away from rejection:

1. **The iPhone Human Interface Guidelines** offer a great example of how essential UI elements should interact and behave.

   We should start by verifying that our Tab Bar, Navigation Bar, and Alert Views work as emphasized by Apple. Many app rejections occur because fundamental UI elements do not work as suggested in the Human Interface Guidelines.

2. Next, we want to make sure that our interface does not mimic form and function of an Apple application that comes pre-installed on iOS, such as *Music*, the *iTunes Music Store*, or the *App Store*.

   Apple tends to pick and choose when to implement this rule, with many web browsers and compasses seeing approval into the store.

3. We'll want to be sure that we're not using trademarks, logos, or a brand identity which we have not been given rights to use.

   Developing an unofficial sequel to our favorite video game may seem like a great idea, but Apple will reject our application if we do not have the rights to use a character or specific image.

   This rule also applies to using icons or artwork that looks similar to iOS system artwork. So for example, if we decided to build an eBook reader, we should refrain from using an icon that could be confused with the *iBooks* icon.

4. We should also guarantee that we do not include excessive swear words, gratuitous sex, or drug use in our application.

   Apple is very adamant about the fact that the *App Store* should be a family friendly place to purchase software, and inappropriate language or crude content could lead to rejection of our application.

   We must also assure that we do not reprogram hardware buttons on the iOS device to serve a function other than their dedicated system wide function. This means that we can't set up the volume up or down button to serve as a shutter button in our camera app, nor could we program the home button to work as a way to fire a weapon in our video game. All device hardware buttons must work as intended throughout our application.

With these tips in mind, we'll be less likely to cross the line and violate Apple's terms of service. Rejection can be costly, so we'll want to guarantee that we don't keep our app from approval because of poor interface decisions.

How it works...

Apple's strict polices may annoy pundits who wish the *App Store* was more open, but the current plans in place are set to help developers achieve greater success. By making every developer comply with specific UI and functional standards, Apple is ensuring a certain level of quality that builds consumer confidence with applications in the *App Store*. Once users trust that an app will work as advertised, they will be more willing to buy apps in the future, which will increase the revenue stream for all developers.

There's more...

When reading Apple guidelines or blog posts about rejection, it can often appear as if Apple discourages innovation and unique interface design. In practice, this is untrue, with Apple offering yearly awards for exceptional app designs that are anything but ordinary.

The Apple design awards

For an example of exceptional design, check out Apple's web page for their yearly WWDC Design Awards `http://developer.apple.com/wwdc/ada/`. Design Award winners typically offer a great example of how we can transform standard interface elements into an exceptional user experience, all while remaining within App Store rules and regulations.

Rejection is a dish best served cold

To help developers better understand application rejection, Apple has created the **Resolution Center** within **iTunes Connect**.

 iTunes Connect is the online web portal where we'll submit and make changes to app binaries. If we want to change the price or availability of our app, we'll head here.

The Resolution Center offers explanations as to why the app was rejected, along with suggestions as to how the application can be modified to comply with Apple policies.

2
Customizing our Icon, the Navigation Bar, and the Tab Bar

In this chapter, we will cover:

- ▶ Designing an application icon and preparing it for the user home screen
- ▶ Creating the rounded edges effect on our icon
- ▶ Removing the app icon's gloss effect
- ▶ Optimizing our newspaper or magazine app's icon for Newsstand in iOS 5
- ▶ Creating a custom Tab Bar for our iPhone application

Introduction

The application icon and essential interaction elements such as the **Navigation Bar** and **Tab Bar** are crucial for the success of our work. The user will be tapping the icon every time they go to use our app, and interact with our navigation elements throughout their entire experience in our application.

If we want success, we must focus on making these components attractive and functional. Attention to detail and the presentation of these pieces will be key, and we'll need to produce our best work if we want to stand out in a sea of apps.

In this chapter, we'll discuss the all-important application icon, along with a couple of other ways in which we can make our work shine on the iPhone, iPod touch, and iPad.

Designing an application icon and preparing it for the user home screen

It's often said that a book shouldn't be judged by its cover, but the harsh reality of mobile development is that an app is often judged by its **icon**. This rounded rectangle will appear on the home screen of every user, and it's important that we create something that is attractive and also a good indication as to what the user should expect after downloading our application.

In this recipe, we'll create a strategy for successful app icon design.

Getting ready

Adobe Photoshop will be our primary tool in the design of our app icon. It may also be helpful to grab some paper and a pencil so that we can sketch out any concepts we may have before we begin working on our computer.

How to do it...

The application icon is a primary component of any work. Appearing in the *App Store*, on a user's home screen, in Spotlight searches, and more, it's an important part of our job.

Let's take a look at several steps that will be useful in the creation of our app icon:

1. We should start by with either a rough sketch or *Photoshop* mockup of our intended design. We should create this mock up at several sizes to help represent the different resolutions at which our icon will be viewed.

2. After we've developed an idea that we believe is going to scale well, its time to sit down in Photoshop or Illustrator and begin work on our icon.

At this point, we need to determine what size canvas we want to design our icon on. Apple requires that our icon be available at a variety of sizes, with a 512 by 512 pixel square currently being the largest required format, but we should be prepared in case this requirement changes in the future and design our icon accordingly. There are two different ways we can go about making our icon "future proof".

We can go about designing the icon in a vector format using an application like *Adobe Illustrator*. Vector drawings will always be the best way to ensure that our icon will scale to any size, but they can be a bit more difficult to create.

If we're more comfortable using a raster image manipulation program like *Photoshop*, it's best to create our icon at a resolution well above what we'll ever need for the *App Store*, starting with a canvas of 4096 by 4096 pixels square or greater.

Such a large raster size will give us a piece of art that will print comfortably on sizes as large as 13 inches when printed at 300 DPI, while also easily scaling down to whatever size we need for the *App Store*.

1. Once we've decided which format we're most comfortable with, its time to go about creating our icon.

2. Once we've completed our icon, it is time to prepare it for inclusion into our application.

3. This icon should then be named `apple-touch-icon.png` and placed inside of our application bundle. iOS will then automatically add the glare effect to the top half of the icon, as seen throughout the interface.

 The `Info.plist` is a file that allows us to customize a bunch of different application attributes. We'll learn how to use it to remove the icon gloss effect in an upcoming recipe titled *Removing the app icon's gloss effect*.

4. After finishing our icon, we may also want to run a small focus group, much like we would in order to gain feedback on our user interface design.

    We can quickly set up a simple website with a form asking for opinions on our design or even email an image of the icon to friends and family in order to facilitate feedback.

When looking to gather opinion on our icon, we want to better understand a user's first impression of our icon. For a good portion of purchase decisions, the icon may be the only bit of insight into our app that the user has before tapping the buy button. We want to make sure that on first impression, the typical user associates our icon with quality, simplicity, and value. If our icon looks amateur, users probably won't consider our application for purchase.

How it works...

Icon design is tough, primarily because we're required to design a small square that represents our application's purpose, quality, and value. It's truly a challenge to design something that works well at 512 pixels and 27 pixels. Let's take a look at how the steps above work together to create a good icon.

Resolution flexibility is arguably the difficult part of icon design, as our work needs to look great at 512 pixels by 512 pixels and at 27 by 27 pixels. Small details that look great at a high resolution can really make an icon indecipherable when scaled down to the lowest resolution required:

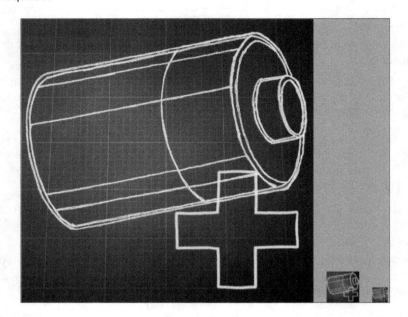

In the above screenshot, we can quickly see how an icon becomes less legible as it decreases in size. It's necessary to provide the icon to Apple in several different sizes, which can vary depending upon the iOS device we're developing our application for and the current operating system requirements from Apple. These file sizes have varied significantly throughout the life of iOS, so we should verify the current requirements in the iOS Development Center before their creation.

Sebastiaan De With keeps an excellent *Photoshop* file for iOS icon design, complete with resolution requirements, which he updates every time Apple changes the icon requirements. We can find the file here at `http://blog.cocoia.com/2010/iphone-4-icon-psd-file/`and it should reference it while designing a new icon.

When building our icon, we should really take time to think about what our icon should look like and what users will think when they first set eyes on it in the App Store. This set process works because it systematically creates a piece of work that will be optimized for the various needs of iOS.

There's more...

It may take a bit of practice to get a firm grasp on what makes a great or poor icon. Here are a few helpful ideas, just in case we're struggling to develop an icon that we're happy with.

Dropping the text

We should always refrain from including a great deal of text in our app icon. Text tends to become illegible when scaled down to small resolutions such as 27 x 27, so it is often best to keep text out of our icon. If we absolutely must include text in our icon, we should use short words that are large in size and in a bold typeface.

Great gradients

From an art design perspective, we'll probably be including an artistic gradient in our icon to offer the illusion of brushed metal or progressive lighting. But choosing a strong color palate for a gradient can be difficult.

Dezigner Folio has created a large library of fresh, modern gradients that they've offered up for free use in any project. For the entire library, feel free to visit their website at `http://www.dezinerfolio.com/2007/05/03/ultimate-web-20-gradients-v30-release`.

If all else fails....

If we're having a rough time with icon design and all else fails, we can always hire a freelance artist or design firm to help out with the production of our application icon. A quick search of Google can help us find a multitude of artists who have become specialists in the field of icon design.

Finding a talented designer can actually be quite affordable, with many freelance artists charging a hundred dollars or less for a high quality icon. As icons can be produced in *Photoshop*, local graphic designers or students can help out at affordable rates as well.

See also

> ▸ *Starting with the sketch in Chapter 1*
> ▸ *Migrating to the high-resolution Retina display in Chapter 1*

Creating the rounded edges effect on our icon

The raised, rounded rectangle bezel is a common trait on many application icons. Made popular by developers such as **Electronic Arts**, **Lima Sky**, **Gameloft**, and others, such icons often look as if they almost have a wooden or metal frame.

Let's take a look at how we can go about creating our own rounded edge effect so that our icons stick out on the *App Store*.

Getting ready

For this recipe, we'll need a copy of **Adobe Photoshop** or another similar raster image editing application. It will also be useful to have the source file, titled `IconBezel.PSD`, to be downloaded from the Packt website.

How to do it...

Creating a **rounded bezel effect** on our icon is relatively simple; we'll just have to work in some rounded rectangles and proper sizing requirements. Let's take a look at the simple steps that we must take to create such an icon:

1. Create a new Photoshop file for the icon, square in shape, measuring at least 512 pixels by 512 pixels. Then, give a color to the background of the file, ideally close in color to our bezel.

 The outer bezel is often styled to look like metal when used in an icon, but we could try to make it look like wood, plastic, or some other material. Be creative and design something unique!

2. Use the Rounded Rectangle tool with a radius of 25 pixels to create a rounded square that fills the entire screen. When we're done, the rounded rectangle should fill the entire square from edge to edge.

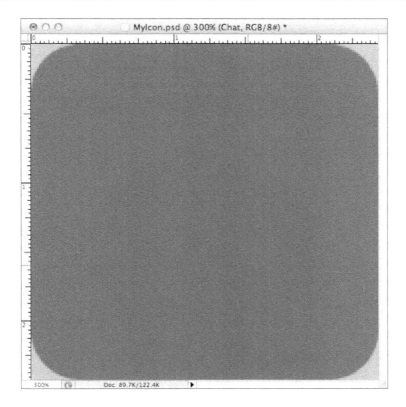

3. Create another second rounded rectangle with a radius of about 15 pixels inside the first rectangle to create desired width bezel.

4. Use a bevel and outer glow to create the illusion of a bezel.

5. Include the desired art in the center of the icon frame.

6. From here, we can save the icon as a PNG in whatever size we need for the app or marketing purposes.

How it works...

On an iOS device's home screen or in the *App Store*, Apple has designed icons to be presented with a rounded edge look. So while we'll create a square piece of art, our icon will look better if we design a bezel or other piece designed around the understanding that our icon will stand apart from the crowd.

Creating the ideal bezel effect isn't easy. For example, in step three, we need to create a second rounded rectangle inside the first. This rectangle should be in a different color from the first, offering a background for art that we'll place in later. It will also contrast with the first rectangle and give the illusion of a bezel.

As shown in the previous screenshot, this second smaller rectangle should have a radius between 10 to 15 pixels. If we use a radius equal to the larger rounded rectangle, our bezel will look somewhat misshapen.

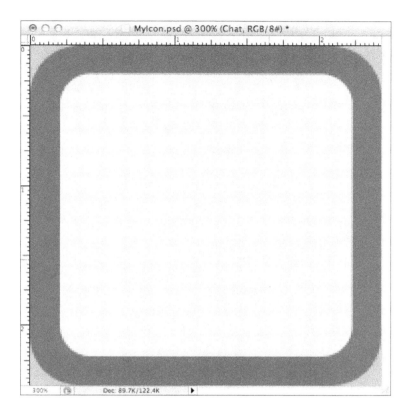

Diving further into the design, by using the **Bezel** and **Emboss** blending effect in Step 4, we'll create a sense of depth that gives the illusion of a bezel, thanks to the **Outer Glow** blending effect on the inner rectangle.

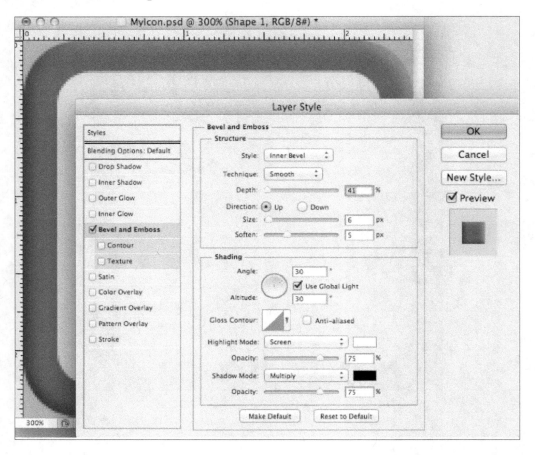

A 6-pixel large inner bevel with a softness of 5 pixels should be fine, but we can play around with these values to create a desirable look. If we're looking to create a metallic look, we may want a greater bevel. If we're creating a wood look, we may want less of a bevel.

For this example, a glow with a size of 6 pixels offers just the shadow necessary to create our desired effect. Like the bevel though, we may want to play with this depending on our desired effect.

The rounded bezel is an easy way to make our icon pop; it just requires that we have an understanding of how our icon will be displayed on a device. With a bit of practice and experimentation, we can design an exceptional application icon.

There's more...

We'll probably be creating a PNG image of our icon to place inside our app and submit to the store, but we shouldn't be including transparencies.

Not being caught cutting corners

A somewhat troubling problem is found in many app icons, where there is noticeable clipping in the corner of icons in the *App Store* and when placed on the device. To an icon with this problem, it looks as if the corners have been cut off a bit and replaced with white pixel artifacts.

This usually occurs when the icon designer creates a bezel like we've built in this recipe, but they don't place a background color in the image under the bezel and instead leave the corners transparent.

 This is a great example as to why we should always test our designs on actual devices before we ship our app. This is a common mistake that could easily be corrected if we tested our icon file on an actual iPhone or iPad.

What happens is, corners aren't accurately sized and the corners aren't filling the entire file properly. The *App Store* and iOS can't properly display transparencies, so these missing pixels appear white and are often in contrast with our designed bezel.

Always include a full square image and use a color background in the corners, even though the user will never see these pixels. This will help to prevent this problem.

See also

▶ *Designing an application icon and preparing it for the user home screen in this chapter*

▶ *Removing the app icon's gloss effect in this chapter*

Removing the app icon's gloss effect

Apple created iOS to offer a standard icon, originally equal to 57 pixels by 57 pixels. On top of these icons, a standard **glass reflection effect** was placed on top of all icons.

But there will be times at which we feel that our icon will look better without the gloss effect. In this recipe, we'll discuss how we can remove this effect and create a crisp and bright icon.

Getting ready

For this recipe, we'll need **XCode** installed on a **Macintosh computer**. We'll also need the project file for our application in order to edit its `Info.plist`.

How to do it...

With a few simple steps, we'll easily remove the ship from our iOS icon on the user's home screen. Let's take a look at what is needed in order to remove the effect:

1. Open our application project in *XCode*. We should begin by opening our project in *XCode*. If we need to check the code out of a repository or just open it from our computer, we should do so now.

2. In *XCode*, open the project's `Info.plist` file. The location of this file may vary based on our application, but it will be present somewhere in the project folder.

3. Add a new row to the Plist and set the key to **Icon already includes gloss effect**.

4. Next, we'll need to create a new row in the Plist and then set the key of that row to the **Icon already includes gloss** value.

5. Set the Boolean value to **YES**, save, and compile our application.

The next time we compile our application, the shine will no longer be present and our app icon will look crisp on the home screen.

 There is no rule with regards to when we should or should not include the gloss effect. Try out both styles to see which suits our icon best.

How it works...

Our application's `Info.plist` file holds a variety of application properties, including the ability to remove the gloss effect from an icon when displayed on the iOS device home screen.

As learned in steps 4 and 5, this Boolean value determines if the gloss effect is placed upon our icon or not. By hovering over an existing row, we'll see a small plus icon that we can click with our mouse in order to create a new row:

Key	Type	Value
Localization native development region	String	en
Bundle display name	String	Hero Defense
Executable file	String	${EXECUTABLE_NAME}
Icon file	String	icon.png
Bundle identifier	String	
InfoDictionary version	String	6.0
Bundle name	String	${PRODUCT_NAME}
Bundle OS Type code	String	APPL
Bundle creator OS Type code	String	????
Bundle version	String	1.3

iOS parses the plist when installing the application, and such settings are then applied to the icon in code by the operating system. It doesn't require much work on our part, and can help make our icon stand out as exceptional.

See also

▶ *Designing an application icon and preparing it for the user home screen in this chapter*

▶ *Creating the rounded edges effect on our icon in this chapter*

Optimizing our newspaper or magazine app's icon for Newsstand in iOS 5

With iOS 5, Apple has developed a new set of application icon attributes to help make our periodical stand out in the new Newsstand feature. Our icon can now look different than the standard glossy rounded rectangle, allowing for our work to gain greater attention from our users.

In this recipe, we'll look at different ways in which we can customize our periodical icon in Newsstand.

Getting ready

In this recipe, we'll need a nearly completed periodical application for which we can complete the necessary icon files. It's important that we have an idea about what sort of art direction will be required for the icon as we complete this work.

How to do it...

Creating icon files for periodicals in iOS 5 and beyond is a bit more complex than the standard application, as we have the ability to have customizable covers that change as content changes with new issues in the app. We can also dress up our app icon to look like a real magazine or newspaper, which can offer neat artistic flare as well. Let's take a look at the steps required to create a periodical icon in iOS 5:

1. Create a standard iOS icon square for the app, measuring 57 and 114 pixels for the iPhone and 72 pixels for the iPad.

2. Design a periodical specific default cover image to appear in Newsstand. Select a binding edge and binding type for the Newsstand cover.

3. Include cover images in future updates to the periodical for inclusion in Newsstand.

When these four steps have been accomplished, our icon will be ready to go for the Newsstand feature in iOS 5.

How it works...

Throughout the history of iOS, designers have only needed to put together a single icon, consisting of a 512-pixel square that is then scaled down to other sizes as required. This made icon design simple and easy, although it was quite difficult to make an icon stand out from the crowd. With iOS 5 and Newsstand, periodicals can now add a bit of customization to help an app's content stand out.

In step one, we'll be designing a standard square icon that will turn into a rounded rectangle and look like any other app icon in iOS. This will be required for our periodical, even though we have new and improved cover icons in Newsstand. The standard icon will be used in the *App Store*, when searching for an app in Spotlight, in the *Settings* application, and in notifications throughout the operating system, so it is required that we still include it in our app binary.

With step two, we'll be designing a more periodical specific icon to serve the purpose of a cover page for our magazine or newspaper when in the Newsstand feature. As new issues come out, we'll be able to update the icon to represent the day or week's cover story, but we'll still need a general periodical cover to display in case we have no updated periodical cover to display. This should be in the art style of our periodical and look much like a standard issue would appear on a physical paper or magazine.

For step three, we'll need to apply binding properties to the cover in the application's `Info.plist`. For the `UINewsstandBindingType` key, we'll provide a string of either `UINewsstandBindingTypeNewspaper` or `UINewsstandBindingTypeMagazine`. This choice is fairly self-explanatory and based on our selection, our periodical cover will look more like either a glossy magazine or a newspaper.

Next, we'll set the `UINewsstandBindingEdge` key to `eitherUINewsstandBindingLeft`, `UINewsstandBindingEdgeRight`, or `UINewsstandBindingEdgeBottom`. With our selection, the periodical cover will be edited to look as if the binding fold is on the left, right, or bottom of the issue.

Finally, we'll need to include updated periodical cover art images whenever we update our application so that iOS can adjust the cover accordingly in Newsstand. This will allow our periodical to appear up to date and grab the user's attention with an updated cover based on our most up-to-date app content.

By following these four steps, our icon will be ready for display in iOS 5's Newsstand feature.

▶ *Designing an application icon and preparing it for the user home screen in this chapter*

▶ *Creating the rounded edges effect on our icon in this chapter*

▶ *Removing the app icon's gloss effect in this chapter*

Creating a custom Tab Bar for our iPhone application

While we'll often want to implement a standard **Tab Bar**, there may be an occasional situation for which we will want to create a customized Tab Bar that offers up a bit of a different look.

This will require that we create the new bar entirely in **Photoshop**, and then use these buttons to transition through different views. As we're creating something custom, we don't have many rules to follow. However, we should still create a Tab Bar that is somewhat recognizable to the user.

In this recipe, we'll discuss a technique for creating a custom Tab Bar for our iPhone application.

Getting ready

For this recipe, we'll need a copy of *Adobe Photoshop* or another similar raster image editing application. It will also be useful to have the source file, titled `TabBar.PSD`, downloaded from the Packt website.

How to do it...

We will need to go about creating a very structured and organized set of image files in order to have an effective custom Tab Bar. Let's take a look at the steps that we'll need to follow:

1. Create a new file in *Photoshop* for the Tab Bar, that is equal to 98 pixels in height and 640 pixels in width. Give a background color to the Tab Bar to what we desire non-active tabs to be in color.

2. Now, we should create a background color in our file that will serve as an inactive tab color background.

3. Next, we should use the guide tool in *Photoshop* to create verticial guidelines to guide where we will place each tab. Guides can be found by selecting **View** in the **Menu Bar** and then choosing **New Guide**.

We'll find the width of each tab by taking the width of the screen and dividing it by the number of tabs that we intend to include. As seen below, if we want to include four tabs here, each tab should be 160 pixels in width on the Retina display.

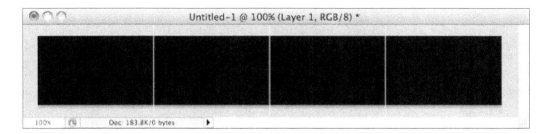

4. For each section of Tab Bar, create active and inactive states for each tab.

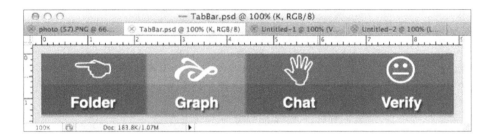

5. Now we need to go about exporting each button for both states. It is typically easiest to go about selecting a single tab using the Marquee tool, and then copy the content from all layers using the **Merge Copy** tool with the *Shift+Command+C* shortcut. We can then create a new file, paste, and save it in both Retina and standard resolutions.

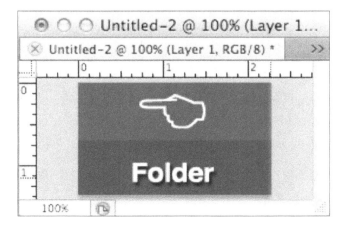

6. As we save an image for each state, we should be sure to use clear file names for each tab, such as `TabOneActive.png` and `TabOneInactive.png`, to help us easily label and make changes to the tabs as need be through development.

7. Place the images as buttons inside of our application. When an inactive tab is tapped, transition to the view that is represented by this tab and change the previous view's tab to the inactive image.

With this method, we'll quickly and easily create a unique Tab Bar that still behaves similar to how the user anticipates the behavior of the standard interface element to be.

How it works...

While a bit more rare, custom Tab Bars can help make our application stand out. The design principles behind the bar are quite simple, so it isn't difficult to re-create through some creative interface work.

In Step 1, we created a file with a resolution of 98 pixels by 640 pixels, because this is Apple's recommended height for the bar, but we really have the creative freedom to do whatever we want with regards to height.

As we move forward in the process, we will create the art for each tab. As we're creating a custom bar, color, texture, button requirement, and other attributes aren't really required to have any specific look. We should keep a general look that remains somewhat familiar to the user, but we should still feel free to use a little creativity.

Once we export our new images, the new Tab Bar is ready to be placed as individual buttons anchored to the bottom of our application interface. We'll create as many buttons across the bottom of the screen as tabs we want, and then create a system through which each view is presented by tapping an inactive button on the bottom of the screen. When this inactive button is tapped, the view will change and the previously active tab button will change to its inactive counterpart.

Remember that if we do decide to go this route, we should still keep the standard Tab Bar behavior intact. We'll be creating something that users won't be expecting and in most situations, that's OK. But since the custom bar will look a bit foreign, we don't want to completely scare away users from something that both looks and behaves completely unexpected.

But through creating something as shown, we can greater customize our interface and make our application our own.

There's more...

In this recipe, we've recommended a height of 49 pixels for a Tab Bar, but is this a requirement? Let's take a look at to why we should follow this rule.

Losing the freshman 15

Our initial desire may be to make our Tab Bar a bit bulkier than the Apple native bar, giving users a bit larger of a tap zone to switch between tabs. This is a bit undesirable, as it can often be confusing to the user and could lead to possible interface problems down the road.

Through day-to-day use of the iPhone, iPad, or iPod touch, the user is going to become trained with regards to what the standard size of a Tab Bar should be. If our bar is much larger or smaller, we'll break the cognitive expectation for the user and they'll not know how to perceive the item at first.

We also need to be aware that Apple could very well change the screen size of the iPhone or iPad, create a new Tab Bar style with different function expectations, or design some other fundamental operating system change. By making our custom Tab Bar similar in size to the original bar, we'll be able to quickly adapt our app if something changes in the future.

See also

▶ *Providing variety through a Tab Bar in Chapter 4*

3
Different Ways to "View" our Application

In this chapter, we will cover:

- ▶ Properly utilizing modal views
- ▶ Getting quick updates with Alert Views
- ▶ Improving our application through table views
- ▶ Integrating the web view into our app
- ▶ Including Twitter in iOS 5
- ▶ Determining which view is better for our app

Introduction

Views controllers are an essential part of iOS development, providing a gateway for users to observe and manage essential data stored inside of an application. These controllers come in many shapes and sizes, and all go about helping users see and control data on screen.

As interface designers, it will be our job to select the appropriate interface element or screen view to properly portray our app interface. To create a top app, we're going to need to stock our interface arsenal with a variety of tricks including **Alert Views**, **Table Views**, and **Web Views**.

 Views are a portion of the iOS screen that are dedicated to organizing photos, text, or other content on screen.

In this chapter, we'll define the different views that make up our user interface and ways to optimize our design through proper implementation of each available option.

Properly utilizing modal views

iOS is a highly **modal** operating system, forcing one application at a time upon the user. Not only are we limited to one application, but we're also limited in space and possible views at any given time when inside our application.

In this recipe, we'll define modal views and the role they play in our application.

Getting ready

Modal views are more prevalent and easy to distinguish on the iPhone and iPod touch, so we should look to have one of these two devices on hand. Modal views do occur on the iPad as well, so it would be helpful to also have this device if possible.

How to do it...

Apple has devised several different modal views for our disposal. One modal view only works on the iPhone, only three work on the iPad, and one can be used on either platform. Let's take a look at the different modal view types available to us:

1. We're given a **full-page** modal view similar to modal views on the iPhone or iPod touch, where the only option on screen is to complete or cancel the modal presentation.

2. A blue Alert View that appears in-app, or out of app as a Push or Local Notification, is also a way to present modal information. **Alert Views** can appear on either the iPhone or iPad.

3. A second popular modal view on iPad is the **Form Sheet**, where the modal view is placed on top of the current window at a fixed size of 540 pixels by 620 pixels. When in the Form Sheet, viewable window space below the modal view is dimmed to visually indicate to prevent the user from interacting with anything other than the modal view. Composing a new email on the iPad is an example of a Form Sheet.

4. A **Page Sheet** is similar to the Form Sheet and also only available on the iPad. While the Form Sheet has a fixed size, the Page Sheet has a fixed width of 768 pixels and a height that spans the entire length of the iPad.

5. A final modal view, also limited to only the iPad is the **Current Context** modal view. In this view, modal content is presented in a split pane or Popover view, filling the entire interface element.

By using any of these modal presentations, we'll be able to offer a linear presentation of data and direct the user towards the most important aspects of our application. The variety of view types offers flexibility, so that we can fine tune our app and create the best experience possible.

How it works...

Modal views allow our application design to present a single functionality to the user at a given time, focusing the user on the specific task at hand. In a traditional computing environment, this sense of modality is less important as we're given a great deal of space on screen to work with and can space application interface functions and interactive well enough in a clear way without forcing the user to attend to a single function at any given time.

Proper understanding of modal views in iOS is essential due to limited device real estate. On a desktop application, large monitors make it easy to refrain from using modal views. However, most information entry scenarios on iPhone or iPod touch devices require modal interfaces in order to make data entry simple and clear.

 For a simple definition, a **modal view** is any view that requires action before the user can move onto another window or view.

When presented with a modal view, the user typically has the choice between entering a piece of data or canceling the action. Sending a text message in the *Google Voice* application is an example of a modal view, as shown below:

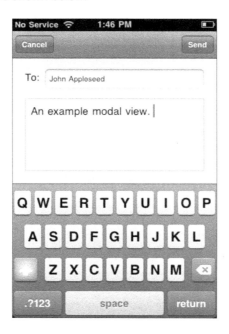

As shown in the following screenshot, picking a local city in *Weather*, composing a new message in *Mail*, and various options in the *Settings* application are all modal interfaces that would not commonly require a modal presentation in a traditional computer setting:

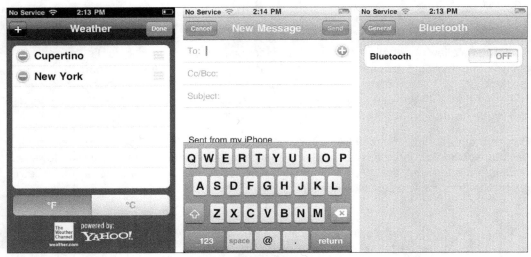

Weather - © 2007-2011 Apple Inc.

Despite the larger screen size, modal views are prevalent on the iPad as well, though not quite as necessary as on the smaller predecessor. On the large device, we're somewhat limited in how we can present our modal view.

Apple has also designed several standard animations to help best integrate modal views. The most common and default modal presentation animation is a **vertical slide** from the bottom of the screen, where the view rises up to take over the viewable area. This standard implementation works well in nearly every scenario and we should implement it if we're uncertain.

The second modal transition style is the **flip**, which makes the view appear as if the transitioned screen exists on the back of the previous screen. When we cancel or close this modal view, the screen flips back around and we're presented with our first screen. Apple's *Weather* application is a great example of this technique, utilizing the flip when transitioning to the location selection page of the application.

The third and final animation is the **page curl** transition, where the corner of the screen flips up to present the user with several application options. When the user has completed or canceled the modal task, the corner curls back down and the original view is presented again. The *Maps* application includes a great example of the curl animation.

Maps - © 2007-2011 Apple Inc.

Modal views will often be a key component in our application, allowing us to focus our user's attention in order to create an easy to understand interface. By integrating standard modal view animations and expected use cases into our application, users will feel familiar and be at home inside of our work.

There's more...

What if we wanted to present a modal view inside of a modal view? Would this be possible in iOS?

Dual modalities

It is possible to offer a modal view that is a child of another modal view inside iOS. For example, when inside a modal view for the composition of a new email, we could tap on the plus icon to pull up a modal view that allows the selection of a contact from the device's address book.

Such a technique is not extremely common and should be used with caution, as this can often create a more complex interface. The most useful scenario for such use is when our initial modal view requires a good deal of data entry and we can help speed the user through this process by automatically adding data in some way.

One important interface note to remember is that if we're looking to build a modal view into another modal view, we can't use the page curl animation. The slide up and flip animation allow for a modal view inside of a modal view, but the page curl does not.

Getting quick updates with Alert Views

System wide notifications are an essential component of any modern mobile operating system, allowing for a quick way to present short text prompts to the end user.

Apple has built **Alert Views** into the iOS SDK, giving developers the same notification system used by Apple for system alerts such as text messages. We can use these several ways, either in application or outside of the application through **Push Notifications** or **Local Notifications**.

In this recipe, we'll break down different ways that we can present the notifications to our user through Alert Views.

Getting ready

Alert Views can be found in many applications on both iPhone and iPad devices. It's useful to have an application on hand like *Alarm Clock*, so that we can test out this view type.

It would also be useful to have *Urban Airship's* website on hand, which can be found at `http://urbanairship.com`. *Urban Airship* is a tool that allows for the easy implementation of notifications into our app. By using their API, we can quickly integrate Push Notifications.

It will also be useful to have a copy of the iOS Human Interface Guidelines on hand and available as well. These guidelines give the most up-to-date information on how Alert Views should be integrated into our app, and can be found online at `http://developer.apple.com/library/ios/#documentation/userexperience/conceptual/mobilehig/Introduction/Introduction.html#//apple_ref/doc/uid/TP40006556-CH1-SW1`. In iOS 5, Apple made a variety of changes to the notification system and also to the implementation of Alert Views. We should famaliarize ourselves with these changes and their impact on Apple's expectations for our interface, as dictated in the official guidelines.

How to do it...

As these notifications are available to every application, even important system notifications such as low battery life warnings, it's important that the user does not tire from excessive alerts. We can also use Alert Views as a way to provide a modal prompt to the user, however, notifications will be the most common use of the view.

In iOS 5, Apple worked extensively to make notifications less intrusive and more mainstreamed into the operating system. By default, notifications now appear in a 40 pixel tall banner that spans across the top of the device screen.

Even with this new and clean presentation, we will still want to refrain from notification overload. In order to assure that our notifications are prompt and appropriate, Apple offers the following suggestions:

- ▶ Alert Views are unnecessary if used to provide an alert for a standard feature of the application. We should reserve these views for the ordinary user notification and for information updates that are essential parts of the application; we should instead try to integrate this data into our standard application interface.

- ▶ Alert Views should never be used to note to the user that the application is functioning or progressing as normal, such as if the application is downloading updated information in the background.

- ▶ We should do our best to avoid Alert Views as a way to confirm an action that the user is looking to perform, even if that action is destructive. If the user is looking to delete an important piece of information and we think it's important to secure confirmation before performing the action, we should use an Action Sheet instead.

- ▶ We should not use Alert Views to inform the user about an action over which they have no control of, such as the inability to connect to a web service or data server. Instead, we should integrate this information into our standard interface.

How we word the text that comprises our title and body of an Alert View is also significant. We're given only a sentence or two as a way to clearly indicate the action that the Alert View represents, along with the consequences of the action. If we're looking to optimize text copy in our alert, we should observe the following:

- ▶ Our Alert View title and body text should be sufficient enough to indicate to the user as to what action is taking place inside the application and what outcomes will occur if a button is pressed.

- ▶ Title text should never exceed a line in length if possible, and should never be single word entries consisting of **Error**, **Warning**, or another vague and unhelpful phrase.

- ▶ Text included inside the Alert View should never directly refer to or call out a user. We should refrain from using words such as you, your, or me.

- ▶ Users of iOS do not have a mouse as an interface device; so we should instruct the user to tap the application, not click.

> ▶ Our text should be succinct enough to fit properly on screen in both portrait and landscape device orientations.

These tips will help us use the Alert View to provide valuable information to our user in a quick and simple way, regardless as to whether we use the alert within our application, through Push Notifications, or in a Local Notification.

How it works...

Alert Views have been designed by Apple to be an unobtrusive, quick way for the operating system to provide feedback to the user about important information that affects an application on the device. Through a quick pop-up banner anchored to the top of the screen in iOS 5 or centered large window in iOS 4 and below, users can receive a text message or be informed about low battery power on the device.

From an interface development point of view, Alert Views are presentable using a narrow and long banner that is anchored to the top of the screen, allowing the user to quickly keep up with system tasks while remaining focused on the task at hand. A short additional message body can also be included inside the Alert View, however it is not a requirement.

 Alert Views have a unique property in that they can be displayed when the user is inside and outside of our application.

In iOS 3.0, Apple gave developers the ability to send out user notifications when in other applications through a server connection called Push Notifications. Push Notifications are relatively difficult to integrate into our application, requires a somewhat costly server solution, and we're limited in the fact that the user must be connected to the Web through WiFi for cellular network to receive the alert.

With iOS 4.0, Apple introduced Local Notifications, which allow us to present a similar Alert View to the user without an Internet connection. However, we're limited in the sense that we can't pull from the Web to offer dynamic alert information such as sports scores or friend messages from a social network.

Neither Push Notifications nor Local Notifications provide a perfect solution, but both are manageable and allow us to keep our application salient to the user. If we're looking to inform our user of an upcoming event or news update, these Alert View styles can be greatly beneficial to our application.

When implementing Alert Views in our application, or when outside our application through Push Notifications or Local Notifications, it's important that we do not overload our user with a flood of alerts. Apple suggests that we limit the amount of notifications that we present to our user, to ensure that such alerts attract the user's attention and do not become a nuisance.

The notification consistency is a strong way to help simplify the entire operating system's interface for the user, while also offering the ability to provide a vast amount of information in a readily available way.

There's more...

Push Notifications can be somewhat difficult to implement into our application, due to complicated server requirements. Luckily, one service looks to simplify the process of adding notifications into our app.

Pushing it back

Urban Airship, found online at `http://urbanairship.com/`, is a great way to go about adding Push Notifications or In-App Purchases into our iOS application.

Urban Airship is a mobile service that offers an API to help integrate necessary frameworks into the application so that we can go about sending a quick Alert View to our user over a network connection. Their web app handles all of the required server backend for notifications, along with accompanying code to help easily integrate Push Notifications into our app.

With modest pricing plans and a fully managed server backend, we'll be hard stretched to find an easier way to integrate the functionality into our work.

See also

- ▸ *Improving our application through Table Views in this chapter*

Improving our application through Table Views

Table Views are an essential component of iOS and an extraordinarily simple way to separate data on screen and give the user an easy way to sort through piles of information.

There are a couple of ways that we can present **Table Views** on screen, with each offering benefits in specific scenarios. In this recipe, we'll discuss several ways in which we can improve our application through Table Views.

A Table View is a single column of information presented on an iOS device as a list of a set of two or more rows.

Getting ready

Table Views are one of the most common ways to go about designing an application on iOS, with prominent applications such as *Music* and *Contacts* being built on the view type. For this recipe, it will be useful to have an iOS device to hand along with some scratch paper to quickly sketch out table flow charts as well.

How to do it...

In their **iOS Human Interface Guidelines**, Apple offers suggestions on which types of Table Views are best for specific use cases. As per their suggestions, here is how we should handle specific functions:

- ▶ If we're using a Table View to provide a list of possible options that the user can choose from, we can use either a plain or grouped view
- ▶ If we're looking to provide several groups of highly distinguishable data on screen, the Grouped Table View is the best option
- ▶ If users will be sorting through a great deal of data where an alphabetical index can help facilitate information lookup, the Plain Table View is the best option because we can include an index to the right of the table
- ▶ If we're presenting hierarchical information to the user, a Plain Table View offers arguably the best way to present a single successive list

Apple also offers other general suggestions for our use of Table Views. These guidelines apply to both grouped and plain views, and can help make our information more accessible to a user:

- ▶ Animations should be used when making edits or when deleting data. This provides a strong sense of visual feedback to the user and makes it more evident that the data is being manipulated on screen
- ▶ If we're presenting a good deal of data on our table, we should avoid waiting until all data has been loaded to display our table. If possible in our app, this will decrease the perceived time that it will take for our application to load
- ▶ When using a Plain Table View, we should never vary the height of our cell. When used, it will often make data feel improperly placed and difficult to manage
- ▶ When possible, we should ensure that our text inside of a cell is brief in order to avoid truncation of important context words

If we adhere to Apple's suggestions for Table Views, we'll find it easy to present a great deal of data to our users in a small amount of space.

How it works...

Table Views are an extremely popular application view because they offer such data flexibility. If we only have a few entries to present to our users, a Grouped Table View will offer an attractive way to present several options. If we have hundreds of data points, a Plain Table View offers a fast and smooth option as well.

If we imagine that Table Views work much like a spreadsheet with rows and columns, it's easy to see how the view offers quick and legible movement up throughout many columns of data. We can move back and forth, offering our users great flexibility.

Luckily for us, Apple has built this powerful framework for us from the ground up, which we can easily integrate into our application design.

There are a variety of native examples in Apple developed applications that we can pull from to learn more about Table Views. In the *Music* application, a Table View is used to list artists or albums. In *Contacts*, a Table View is used to sort through the list of stored contact information. When we're viewing the top 25 listings in the *App Store*, Table Views are used to sort that information as well.

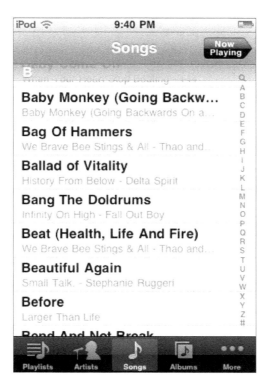

Plain Table Views are the simplest of Table Views, with rows that span from one side of the iOS device screen to the other. As shown in the previous screenshot, songs in *Music* are a great example of a Plain Table View, offering one song per row that spans the entire screen in width.

We can make slight modifications to these views as well, offering the ability to customize the cell to include multiple lines of data and even images. Plain Table Views are perfect for a large number of rows, where we want to give users the ability to flip through data quickly. Data inside Plain Table Views can also be given header information or sorted quickly, offering more flexibility in presentation.

Settings - © 2007-2011 Apple Inc.

Grouped Table Views are another valuable type of view for use in our application. Using this interface element, a slight padding is given between the edge of the screen and the table row. As shown in the previous screenshot from the **Settings** application, Grouped Table Views are often useful when dealing with fewer objects that work well being grouped into specific categories. These groups are laid out on top of a blue and white grid pattern by default, but this background is customizable and can be changed if we think a different pattern would work better with our design.

There's more...

While we didn't discuss it in depth in this recipe, Plain Table Views often go hand in hand with Navigation Bars. If we're looking to include this view inside our app, we may want to consider the Navigation Bar as well.

Two peas in a pod

Navigation Bars and Plain Table Views work well together because the Navigation Bar allows for quick navigation back and forth through different tables. If we'd like to offer further detail on a table object, we only need to allow the user to tap on an entry then jump forward into a further view.

The two work perfectly together if we consider the Navigation Bar to be header columns in a spreadsheet, with data inside the table cells taking the role of rows.

If the user taps upon a table cell, it's much like moving to the next column. Hitting back on the Navigation Bar is like moving back a column.

Using this metaphor, it's easy to understand how users can quickly move through a great deal of data.

See also

▸   *Getting quick updates with Alert Views in this chapter*

Integrating Web View into our app

Being connected to the Internet at any given moment with a full web browser is really a factor that helped propel the iPhone's massive popularity. While browsing on a mobile device wasn't exactly a new concept when the phone first released, no manufacturer had ever put together such a smooth experience.

This power web browser was built on Apple's **Web Kit** rendering engine, which provided an experience similar to what was possible on *Safari* for OS X. Rich web content was already available out of the box and with a bit of code modification, any website could be optimized for the small screen.

In compiling the first public version of the iOS SDK, Apple gave the developers access to Web Kit through a **Web View**. In this recipe, we'll discuss different ways to go about including Web Views inside our application.

Getting ready

For this application, we should have access to mobile *Safari* on our iPhone or iPad device.

How to do it...

The mobile Safari browser built with Web Kit may have been one of the most significant aspects of the first iPhone release. With mobile *Safari*, Apple built the most complete and feature packed web browser ever to exist on a phone. Without modification, millions of websites were available as they were intended to be viewed and not in a stripped down mobile shell.

In developing the iOS SDK, Apple wisely included easy access in the same Web Kit rendering engine for use inside our applications. Using code to include a Web View in our app, gives a completely contained web engine that allows us to render HTML or load an external web page inside our application.

Web Views can be used in one of two ways inside our application. Let's take a look at the different ways in which we can use this view:

1. **To display local HTML code**: First, we could use the view to display local HTML information stored inside of our application. This can be useful for rich text information, such as an acknowledgements page.

   When propagating our application with data and text inside of a Web View, we can use common HTML page formatting to structure our work. Using common tags, we can make our text bold or italic and modify font color. Web Views can be a great tool for designers new to iOS, as HTML formatting is more common and could be more familiar to those migrating from web design.

2. **To display an external web page within our application**: The second use of a Web View would be to use the view as a way to let our user navigate to a web page without leaving our application. For example, we may create an application that allows a user to quickly find local restaurants. By integrating a Web View, we can give our user the opportunity to view a restaurant web site quickly without ever leaving the application.

 This ability may be the most beneficial use of a Web View from a design perspective that allows us to give our user the ability to quickly surf the web while remaining inside of our application.

By integrating a Web View in our application, we're able to capitalize on Apple's powerful Web Kit rendering engine to provide a dynamic app experience.

How it works...

Being built on top of the Web Kit rendering engine, Web Views allow us to include an extensive range of web technologies natively into our application.

When we implement a Web View into our application, we should be aware that our app will perform much like we're writing code for the Web. HTML will render accordingly, text will format like in a browser, and our application will work much like having Safari embedded into our work. It's also important to note that the Web View will also automatically turn information such as a phone number into a link that will dial the number in the phone application as well.

The view also gives us the great ability to offer access to websites without pushing the user of our app. *Twitter for iPhone* uses a Web View for a similar purpose, allowing users to view links included within tweets without ever being kicked out to the actual *Safari* application. As shown below, this keeps the user from the frustrating experience of frequently switching applications while still offering a full web experience.

For developers looking to bring their existing web application to iOS, or for designers looking to pull from their previous knowledge of HTML, the Web View is a simple way for developers to expedite development and create quality applications.

There's more...

Even though we're often integrating a Web View into our application and users will often be unaware that they're actually browsing a website, it's important to make the user feel natural while browsing.

Back, forward, and home

If we integrate a standard Web View into the application, we also need to plan a way for the user to navigate through various web pages or web content. If we link to an outside website and the user is navigating, we'll need to design standard web controls into our Web View interface.

At the bare minimum, we need to integrate a way to move back and forward through web pages along with a button to go back into our application if we're pushing the user onto a page on the Internet. These functions should work identically to back and forward buttons found on a standard web browser.

If we have space and capability, adding email functionality for a web address may be another worthwhile feature to include into our Web View as well. If the user finds an interesting page while inside the view, they'll need a way to share it with friends. Because there is no built-in address bar in a Web View, an email function is an easy way for the user to get the link to the page they're viewing while inside of our application.

See also

▶   *Getting quick updates with an Alert View in this chapter*

Including Twitter in iOS 5

In iOS 5, Apple has given application developers the ability to allow the user to send messages over Twitter in a uniform, easily manageable way inside of every application. Much like the ability to draft an e-mail or send a text message natively within an app, users can now tweet much in the same manner.

Twitter is an extremely popular social network, where users post 140 character messages that can be read by anyone across the world. It's currently used by millions of people worldwide.

For this recipe, we'll take a look at the interface requirements that will be required of us if we decide to include Twitter directly into our application in iOS 5.

Getting ready

For this recipe, we'll need the latest version of Apple's developer SDK for iOS 5. This can be downloaded in the iOS Dev Center located at `http://developer.apple.com`.

How to do it...

The ability to integrate native e-mail and SMS controllers inside of our application has always been a strength of iOS, making it easy for developers to integrate such communication features while also providing a consistent and familiar interface for users. With the growing popularity of Twitter, Apple has created away for developers to easily integrate the social network into apps with iOS 5. Let's take a look at how we'll need to account for this in our interface:

1. Determine the type of content that should be eligible for tweets, or when it's appropriate for the user to tweet.

2. Create an interface that allows for the user to initiate the `TWTweetComposeViewController`, making it clear as to what is being included in the tweet.

3. Use the `TWTweetComposeViewControllerResult` property to verify if the tweet was posted correctly, and then display an appropriate message to the user as to the status of their tweet.

Once we complete these steps, we'll have included *Twitter* functionality into our app and users will be able to jump in and tweet from our application.

How it works...

Twitter has become a nearly universal messaging tool, with adaptation rates high among tech savvy iPhone users. The network is a great place to share content, so being able to allow users to inform their friends about our app with ease is an extremely noteworthy feature.

In step one, we need to first decide as to what content inside of our application is suitable for tweeting. This will be a mutual decision between the team members in charge of programming and design, as we'll need to design what parts of our app, be it text, photos, high scores, and the like are even possible to tweet.

Step two is the most difficult in implementing the tweet feature, as we need to design a way in which to invoke the view controller that allows for the user to compose and send a message to *Twitter*. This will need to be a button or some other prompt for the user to begin the tweet process. In the Photos application, a share button in the Toolbar provides an Action Sheet with multiple sharing options, including *Twitter*.

Imagine this step to be much like including an e-mail view or SMS view in an application for iOS 3 or iOS 4 which we may have built in the past. *Twitter* is a form of communication much like these other mediums, so the interface design through which we begin the process of tweeting should be similar.

A choice on an Action Sheet like *Photos* or specific button for tweeting will be sufficient here. As shown below, iOS will take control and allow the user compose a tweet once we've handed over control to the TWTweetComposeViewController.

Finally, we'll need to provide some sort of interface option that makes it apparent to the user that the tweet has been sent off successfully. A quick overlay displaying "Tweet sent successfully" or text placed in line with the content on our interface will be sufficient. We'll just need something that allows the user to look back and realize that they performed all of the steps required to share their work with the world.

Once we're finished with these interface steps, our application will be ready for users to share content using *Twitter*.

There's more...

If *Twitter* is our first foray into content sharing in our app, we may want to expand a bit further and continue to make it easy for users to tell their friends and family about our app.

Keep on giving

In iOS 3 and iOS 4, Apple allowed for us to use email and SMS view controllers in an almost identical manner to that which we walked through in this recipe. If Twitter is the first time we've considered including social networking or easy communication tools into our app, we may want to also go ahead and allow users to email or SMS message their friends about our app in a similar manner to *Twitter*.

By making it easy for users to share information with their friends, they'll be more likely to tell their friends about our work. Recommendations from a peer are one of the leading reasons why people purchase or download an app, so we should make it easy for people to tip off their friends to our work.

Determining which view is better for our app

Between Web Views and Table Views, it can often be difficult to determine which route is best for our application design. While some applications types lend themselves to an obvious view choice, other apps can often work out well with multiple view types.

In this recipe, we'll discuss several Apple developed applications, their view types, and why this choice was best for the application.

Getting ready

For this recipe, we should have an iOS device in order to follow each example application and take note of the view used.

How to do it...

In looking for inspiration as to how to apply the most appropriate view to our work, it's often beneficial to pull from applications developed by Apple. Apple designs are created around proper management of specific view types, and offer exemplary insight into what different views were designed to accomplish.

In the *Settings* application, we're given a strong example of Grouped Table Views. *Settings* offers a variety of different functions to the user, and it must present these options in a quick and easily accessible menu.

Apple's grouped WiFi options together, Apple built application settings together, and then all *App Store* apps together in another group. Tapping on any category pushes forward into deeper device options, with more Grouped Table Views and further options. If we're handling an application where we want to offer the user quick access to a variety of information categories, Grouped Table Views work well.

Grouped Table Views work well when handling data points or options that are of a different category, but what about when we're handling a great deal of information that all falls in the same category?

Music and *Contacts* handle this type of data management with ease by using a Plain Table View. By using the Plain Table View, we can offer a lengthy table full of data in a singular scrolling view. These tables can offer hundreds of entries, listed alphabetically or in another preferable order. By tapping on an entry in the table, we can push the user forward into another view and use a Navigation Bar to allow for quickly moving back to the primary table.

Web Views are used to display rich web content inside the *Mail* application. The Web View works well with email content, because it allows for easy integration of multiple font types or colors as well as clean inclusion of photos. If we intend to pull web content or would prefer to use HTML as a way to format content on screen, the Web View is the best route for our application. As shown below, an image is shown inside the Mail application using HTML as a way to display the image data:

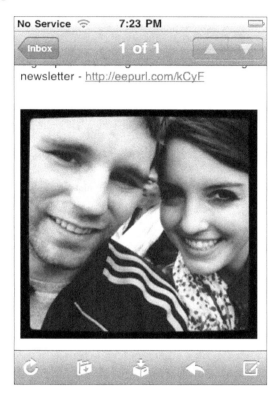

Alert Views are another option that we've covered and could implement into our application as well. As a reminder, Alert Views can be displayed inside our application or outside of the application through use of Push Notifications and Local Notifications.

Apple uses Alert Views heavily through the *Messages* and *Clock* application. Alert Views offer a quick way to give the user notice about a change in our application, but we should use them sparingly as a way to notify the user. It's also important to remember that applications cannot be built using only Alert Views and that these notifications can only be used as a way to build upon our current work. However, if we're looking to occasionally update our user outside of our application, Alert Views are the only option available and they provide a great service to our users. As an example below, the Alarm application uses an Alert View to notify the user that an alarm has gone off:

In iOS 5, Apple drastically altered the way in which Alert Views are presented to the user. In the screen shot above, we can see the iOS 4 and earlier style of notifications. Below, we can see the new iOS 5 default style.

The new Alert View style is obviously much less intrusive and makes it easy for users to keep up with their apps when busy elsewhere. However, we must also keep in mind that at least for the near future, many users will be running iOS 4 and notifications from our app should behave well and in either style.

By using Apple's built-in applications, we can gain a deep understanding as to how Web Views, Table Views, and Alert Views inside of our own work. Whether we're sorting through pages of data, presenting dynamic web content, or alerting our user about an incoming text message, Apple has provided a variety of possibilities inside of their native SDK for our use.

How it works...

Apple's designed each different view type to help provide a platform for a specific type of use case, as a way for us to design detailed applications quickly. Each view may seem limited initially; however by focusing on a specific function, we're given powerful tools for the most common functions we'll need inside of our application.

Working with numerous different view types may seem difficult up front, but once we begin designing and preparing for the limitations of each view type, we'll be well prepared to tie these different capabilities together to create the ultimate iOS application.

We'll find ourselves having some difficulties at first, especially when it comes to understanding exactly which view is capable of specific functionalities. When we're lost, it's best to pull from Apple's bundled applications as an example in order to piece together the methodology they've used to design their work, then use this inspiration as a foundation for our interface design.

See also

> ▸ *Improving our application through Table Views in this chapter*
>
> ▸ *Integrating Web View into our app in this chapter*
>
> ▸ *Getting quick updates with Alert Views in this chapter*

4

Utilizing Common UI Elements

In this chapter, we will cover:

> ▸ Implementing application functionality using a Navigation Bar

> ▸ Providing variety through a Tab Bar

> ▸ Speeding up data entry through pickers

> ▸ Simplicity in the Slider control

> ▸ Offering complex control through an Action Sheet

> ▸ Using UI to keep users inside our application

> ▸ Making text fade in or out of a view

Introduction

We've discussed, in a fair amount of detail, the significance and importance of Apple's native interface elements like the **Navigation Bar** and **Tab Bar**. They're essential components for the development of simple and intuitive applications, and we should make a good effort to go about including them in our application.

Navigation Bars and Tab Bars are the most commonly implemented standard application elements, but tools such as the **Picker** and **Action Sheet** are also helpful when developing an easy to use application. If we're going to implement these tools into our work, we should learn the proper way to go about including such functions in our work. Because these elements come bundled into the SDK, it's important that we understand their fundamental tendencies so that we fall in line with consumer expectations.

In this chapter, we'll discuss the heavily popular elements along with lighter used elements such as the on/off slider. After we work our way through each element, we'll be adding the appropriate feature to our interface with ease.

Implementing application functionality using a Navigation Bar

With the development of iOS, it became necessary for Apple to design a clean and functional way for device users to quickly navigate between huge piles of data.

It's difficult, if not impossible, to offer the same amount of choices and data detail given a 3.5 inch screen. Design concessions from the size constraint have made standard interface elements from a desktop computing environment almost impossible to implement.

The Navigation Bar was an outstanding interface convention to include in the native SDK, allowing developers to easily offer multiple pages of tabled data in an easy to access format. Anchored to the top of the application screen, the bar allows the user to tap onto an on screen item and then quickly move backwards to the previous screen.

In this recipe, we'll take a look at several ways by which we can go about implementing application functionality using a Navigation Bar.

Getting ready

For this recipe, it will be useful to have access to an iOS device with loaded music, so that we can take note of the Navigation Bar inside the *Music* application.

How to do it...

The Navigation Bar is an iOS staple, with prominent interface placement on popular Apple developed applications such as *Music*, the *App Store*, *iTunes*, *Photos*, *Game Center*, *YouTube*, *Calendar*, *Mail*, *Videos*, and more.

 Navigation Bars are a fairly flexible native interface element, offering many opportunities inside of our application. It can be customized to fit nearly any color, attribute, and navigation requirement we may.

The single most important rule that we must follow when including a Navigation Bar into our application, is that the bar must be anchored to the top of the application screen. In no situation can we have the bar floating in the middle of the screen, or anchored to the bottom of the interface.

According to Apple's requirements in the Human Interface Guidelines, the bar also has a fixed height of 44 pixels, which doubles to 88 pixels on a retina display, and always spans across the entire screen regardless as to if the device is in portrait or landscape mode.

Commonly, Navigation Bars are used in tandem with **Table Views**, because it allows for quick movement forward and back between table screens. This is because Apple has developed simple integration of forward and back buttons between data tables. The buttons fit in and animate onto the bar quite easily, offering quick progression. If the user taps upon a table item to learn more, they can quickly tap the Back button and be presented with the previous screen. The following screenshot shows how a Back button is utilized in the *App Store*:

The Navigation Bar is also used to offer quick access to application essential features, as we're not limited to pushing the user forward or backwards a screen view. Ideally our bar will comfortably fit a maximum of two different buttons, with one on the left flank of the bar and the other on the right, and a logo or contextual information about the current view often presented in the middle. As shown in the *Facebook* application below, quick links to the app's home screen and Live Feed are presented in the Navigation Bar:

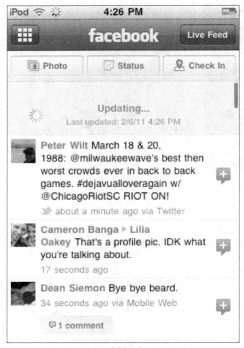

Facebook - © 2011 Facebook Inc.

The Navigation Bar will be a unifying way to connect our user through the collection of views and tools that make up our iPhone or iPad application. We should become familiar with them as soon as possible, as they're one of the few staples that we'll rely upon in a majority of the projects we work on.

How it works...

Applications that make use of the Navigation Bar work well because the 44-pixel bar remains constant while speedy back and forward arrows allow the user to move quickly throughout our application.

The bar serves the same purpose as the front page for different sections to a newspaper, offering an iconic and consistent brand no matter what page we're in, while offering view by view customization to help make each page do its own work.

Visually, the Navigation Bar works because it remains anchored to the top of the screen view and spans the length of the entire screen width. When pushing forward or heading backwards from view to view, standard animations and behavior make it appear as if the content on screen is sliding so that our content lays in wait, ready to fall into position once we make a navigation decision.

 The Navigation Bar can be used to contain a search bar as well, as seen inside of the *Maps* application. The Navigation Bar lives up to its name in this app, giving the users the ability to navigate wherever they would like by typing in their destination in order to be presented with a map.

The Navigation Bar, commonplace inside many applications, makes the bar familiar and our application easy to use, increasing user satisfaction. While it may seem redundant, it's important that we keep navigation in mind when using the Navigation Bar. If we implement it into our application, it should be used to move throughout different views of the interface. When users see the bar anchored to the top of the screen, they'll expect that the bar will be used to help move throughout the application. If we don't use it to provide essential navigation, our interface will be confusing and difficult to manage.

There's more...

We may feel inclined to add a bit of style to our Navigation Bar. Here's a tip to make our work stand out from the crowd.

Adding some style

Simple gradient color Navigation Bars are the default styling, and are commonly found in applications using the element.

However, we can design a pattern or texture to lay upon the Navigation Bar, offering a bit of depth or differentiation while also keeping our application native. For more information about customizing our Navigation Bar, we should check out the *Creating a texture overlay for our Navigation Bar* recipe.

Instagram provides a subtle texture to the Navigation Bar that stands out, while keeping a native appearance as well.

See also

  ▸   *Improving our application through Table Views* in *Chapter 3*

Providing variety through a Tab Bar

The Tab Bar is an extraordinary way to allow quick access to several different modes inside of our application. Each tab can provide a distinct function within the application, which works well when attempting to integrate several distinguishable features into our work.

In this recipe, we'll discuss the key characteristics of Tab Bar navigation based applications. We'll also discuss appropriate uses of the interface element as well.

Getting ready

For this recipe, we should attempt to have access to both an iPhone and iPad, as Tab Bars can vary slightly between devices.

How to do it...

We use the Tab Bar inside of our application due to its ease of integration and structural simplicity for users. Because it's an extremely common element, users will immediately recognize how to use it throughout our app.

The Tab Bar works well between different application functions because it's always salient. No matter what the user does inside of the application, the Tab Bar stays anchored to the bottom of the screen and the user can quickly cycle between functions. This allows for rapid navigation and user freedom between modes.

When using a Tab Bar in its standard form, our design work is fairly simple. However, there are several significant pitfalls that we may fall into if we're not careful, and these problems could ruin our application interface. Let's take a look at important mistakes that we should avoid with our Tab Bar:

- First, the tabs should each cause the user to be presented with a new view.
- We should be careful to never include too many tabs on our Tab Bar.
- While the default color scheme for a Tab Bar is a black gradient with gray or blue icons, there is a precedence to use a different design style if desired. If we're comfortable in making our interface stand out from the crowd, we could follow suit and use a unique Tab Bar color.

If we do decide that quick access to several important application views is necessary for our application, the Tab Bar will be our go to navigation element. We'll find ourselves integrating the bar quite commonly and with a bit of practice, it will be a strong component in our interface design toolbox.

How it works...

Along with the Navigation Bar, the Tab Bar is easily the most commonly used interface element in iOS. Always anchored to the bottom of the screen and available on both the iPhone and iPad, it's a consistent and easy to integrate component.

The Tab Bar is 49 pixels in height, 98 pixels on a Retina display, and can be broken up into two to five tabs. The Tab Bar runs across the length of the device width and is a black gradient in color, with text and icons to distinguish between different pages. The selected and active tab is noted with a lighter gradient rounded rectangle and blue hue to the tab icon:

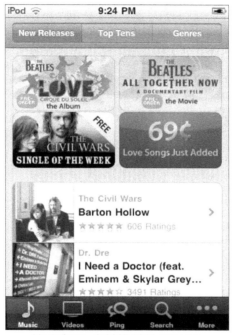

Music Store - © 2007-2011 Apple Inc.

Above, we can see the Tab Bar in the *iTunes* application. The purpose of a Tab Bar is to offer the user quick navigation between several differentiating application functions. Whereas the Navigation Bar is designed to quickly move the user back and forth between pages designed to flow in succession, the Tab Bar is designed around non-linear items.

 A wonderful example of Tab Bar functionality can also be found in Apple's *App Store*, *Game Center*, and *YouTube* applications. In an application such as *iTunes*, tabs offer quick access to the music store, movies store, Ping network, store search, and more.

When it comes to things that we shouldn't do with the Tab Bar, we need to remember the following keys. So long as we avoid these pitfalls, users should remain comfortable in our app:

▶ We should never use a tab as a button to control functions on a current screen view. The bar should always move users between views if it is going to be implemented. In this way, it's important to not confuse a Tab Bar with a Toolbar, which sits in a similar position but contains buttons to control the active view.

▶ Second, it's generally accepted that five tabs is the maximum number of tabs that the iPhone can display properly. For the iPad, there is less of a strict numerical restriction; however Apple advises that we use a reasonable number of tabs. While "reasonable" isn't exactly a quantifiable figure, we should think twice about our interface if we feel that more than six tabs are necessary on an iPad design.

▶ If we have a need for more tabs, we can follow the lead of other applications and use a "more" tab to aggregate multiple application functions when there are not enough tabs to suffice for important application features. As we can see below, *iTunes* is again a great example of this, offering a Table View linking to Podcasts, Audiobooks, iTunes University, and Downloads. If we feel as if we need tabs for more than five items, an aggregate tab can help offer this possibility.

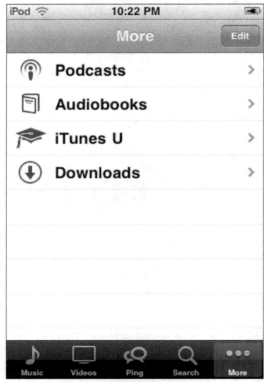

Music - © 2007-2011 Apple Inc.

Finally, Apple offers some standard icons for our inclusion in a Tab Bar, but their selection is hardly exhaustive and we will likely need to create our own icons for our tabs. If we're designing a Tab Bar icon, we should design it using solid black as the icon color, with a resolution of 30 x 30 or 60 x 60 for a retina device. We can create our own custom Tab Bar if we do so desire as well, although we should be careful not to diverge to the extent where we confuse our user due to unfamiliarity.

The default style works well because it offers an elegant and easy to manipulate, persistent presence that serves an important purpose while not over distracting the user.

The Tab Bar's simplicity and subtle placement allow quick access to important screens while not being over bearing. The consistency between applications allows users to gain confidence in our work before they ever even step foot inside of our app.

There's more...

Interface conventions are a valuable tool, and an important guideline to follow when developing our application. However, once we're a bit more comfortable with the standards of iOS interface design, we can begin to diverge a bit within our application interface.

Making our app stand out from the crowd

While Tab Bars are typically black with blue or gray icons, there has been a precedence to add a bit more flair to the presentation.

In Game Center, Apple uses a fake wood styling to offer the look of an old game board. If we have a specific niche for our app that we think would benefit from a unique Tab Bar, we can consider going the Game Center route with our work.

See also

- *Creating a custom Tab Bar for our application* in *Chapter 2*
- *Implementing application functionality using a Navigation Bar in Chapter 4*

Speeding up data entry through pickers and custom keyboards

Data entry is arguably the most mundane and uninteresting aspect of interface design. Regardless as to how you frame it, there is nothing sexy about users entering significant amounts of data.

That being said, exceptional implementation of data entry can be one of the most influential components in successful application design. While mobile computing has grown leaps and bounds in several short years, we still haven't overcome the difficulty that comes along with typing on a 3.5 inch screen.

While we can't increase the size of the keyboard, we can go about implementing pickers and alternative keyboards in order to help make data entry easier on our users. For this recipe, we'll go about discussing several data entry opportunities for our application.

Getting ready

For this recipe, we should prepare by taking note of the various types of data entry we plan to require from the user. We should also have the latest version documentation on custom keyboards from the iOS Developer Center, as this document changes frequently with iOS version upgrades.

How to do it...

There are two important data entry aides that we should include inside of our application whenever applicable: **custom keyboards** and **Picker Views**.

Custom keyboards

We should incorporate iOS's custom keyboard views in appropriate data entry scenarios where such views can help expedite the time it takes for users to quickly key in digits or characters.

For example, Apple offers multiple text keyboard types to help optimize input depending on the text entered. Normally, the iOS keyboard contains a long space bar and characters such as a period or at-sign. However, we can implement the custom Email keyboard when we're composing a message.

Likewise, we can give our web browsing users the custom Web URL keyboard with easy access to a "forward slash" and ".com" button. If our user is entering numerical data, the small digits of the standard keyboard can be difficult to press, so we can increase user productivity and implement the Phone keyboard to help the process.

Apple offers a variety of custom keyboards, and consistently adds new types of keyboard views as they release new versions of iOS. As shown above, Apple provides a variety of keyboards that each serve a unique purpose depending upon our application type. No matter what type of data we're looking to have the user type, there should be an appropriate keyboard to help. If need be, we could also go about creating our own application keyboard type as well if we're adventurous.

Picker Views

Pickers can be set up to help perform a variety of tasks. Apple has created a standard **Date and Time Picker** that helps with entries in applications such as Calendar or Alarm Clock. If we need a specific day or hour from our user, this is probably the preferable method of entry for the user.

A generic Picker allows for any variety of data entry, and can be customized to help out any data entry scenario where we can limit the user to a set number of choices.

In applications like *Lose It*, a Picker View is used to help the user quickly track food intake. In this Picker View screenshot, the user can select a whole number or a fraction, as well as a unit for the food item. It's a quick and painless process, and the user can quickly continue about their business.

How it works...

Custom keyboards are an ideal solution on a touch screen device, because we can create our keyboard in software and give it essentially any functionality we'd like. The same piece of screen real estate reserved for a traditional QWERTY keyboard can quickly be modified to a number pad or special character keyboard.

They're fairly self-explanatory in the sense that they're specially developed keyboards that help the user at entering data for a specific task. While QWERTY keyboards have long been standard these focus on a different task such as number entry or with foreign text characters.

Such specialized views are one significant advantage of a completely touch based mobile interface. Devices with physical keyboards provide tactile feedback, but can't adapt quickly to application needs like a custom view.

Keyboard will always work well with text; it will just depend upon which one we use based on what type of data we expect the user to most commonly enter. If we expect to web surf, it may be best to include a ".com" button. If we plan on entering in a variety of numbers, a keypad may be best. Feel free to experiment with Apple's latest keyboard options to determine what is best given any app interface.

Much like custom keyboards, a Picker View can also greatly benefit our app. A little less obvious but equally valuable, these views help greatly expedite the amount of time it takes to enter in dates, times, or one of the several different choices. The Picker focuses on one specific entry, which is the selected value. Other values are then selectable by swiping a finger up or down on the picker, helping to display previously hidden values.

In the previous screenshot, we don't want to force the user to type in 11:00 P.M. on their keyboard every time they try to schedule an event, so we help speed up this process through the Picker. A quick flick and the user can set the time they desire to place a calendar event.

Likewise, the Picker View is an ingenious solution whose simplicity highlights the revolutionary iOS interface. Through graphical appearance, we can simulate a flickable wheel that contains all necessary choices for a particular data problem.

Picker Views are great when we can minimize the number of inputs that the user will be inserting into any given field, as we can only allow for specific entries to be placed. If we want to know what day of the week is best for a reminder, it doesn't make sense to make the user type out each letter to Friday when we can just have them quickly select it from a Picker list.

Data entry on a mobile phone has always been a difficult design problem. It's difficult, if not nearly impossible, to make entry easy on such a small screen. We're never going to completely solve the problem, but we can definitely use methods such as a Picker View or custom keyboard to help alleviate our user's pain.

Apple's inclusion of these custom components inside of iOS helps create the "magical" interface that draws users to the platform. It's easy for developers to include such elements into our own applications. Because the elements are easy to implement, designers can spend less time focusing on data entry, and more on eye candy and the important attributes of our application's design.

There's more...

Keyboards are a key component to any interface, as they're the mechanism for transferring user text-based commands to the application. Here are a few ways that we can go about making our application more applicable for international users or web users.

Foreign languages can work too

Apple's not just included native keyboard support for English, but for a variety of languages as well. Specifically, they've included strong keyboard support for Chinese and Japanese inside of the operating system.

If we're planning an application with strong international appeal, we may want to guarantee that our application works optimally with multiple device languages as well, as we don't want international users to have a disappointing experience.

Keyboards on the Web

In this recipe, we discuss customizing keyboards for native applications, but what about if we want to customize the displayed keyboard inside of a web app?

The HTML and requirements for doing so require a good bit of web programming, but it's definitely possible with a bit of work. Apple's offered up a guide on how to do so, along with the links to other relevant HTML coding guides, available in the Safari Developer Center at `http://developer.apple.com/library/safari/#codinghowtos/Mobile/UserExperience/_index.html`.

Simplicity in the Slider control

Audio volume, screen brightness, and font size—these three attributes are all important features of a mobile operating system like the iPhone.

We often discuss ways to quickly let our user pick between two different choices. A or B, up or down, left or right, black or white, a mobile interface often relies heavily on limiting the choices in order to optimize usability. But what about scenarios that are a bit more gray?

For example, we don't want to give our user the option between either loud music or no music. Likewise, an extremely bright screen or very dim screen may not be preferable for user readability. There will be situations when the user wants a moderate music volume or medium level of brightness.

When we want to give the user a range of choices between two opposite poles, the **Slider** control may be the most convenient UI element for our application design.

Let's take a look at the Slider element and learn more about how to best integrate it into our work.

Getting ready

For preparation to use a Slider, we should research the implementation of the Slider inside the *Music* application and Brightness page of the *Settings* application.

How to do it...

On a traditional phone with hardware buttons, we would typically use a dial or plus and minus buttons to increase and decrease levels. On iOS, this becomes a problem because there is no physical dial and repetitive button presses are uncomfortable on a glass screen that lacks tactile feedback.

For application control requirements where we would prefer to let the user choose a maximum value, a minimum value, or every value in between, a Slider control is essential.

The controller is simple in nature and requires essentially no explanation to the user. By default, it exists in a straight bar that alights either vertically or horizontally. A small brushed aluminum circle denotes the current position of the Slider and a fill color, typically blue, is found to the left of the selection circle to give a visual cue as a rough idea of how far the one side or the other the Slider is placed. As shown in the following screenshot, standard use for a Slider would be when determining a value like music track volume:

Erratic movement of the Slider or scale changes that do not feel smooth will make our application feel choppy and poorly programmed, as users will compare the experience to Apple's native use of the element. Because of this, it's essential that we have an ideal experience. If our application can't smoothly institute a Slider, we may be best suited to find a different interface element for the application function.

How it works...

Sliders work well on iOS because they're a wonderful **skeuomorphic** tool that offers an infinite range of possibilities in a seemingly one-to-one ratio, mimicking a real life dial or lever. The further I go in one direction or another, the closer I am to the limit value that presides at the end of the switch.

For the Slider to work, there should be a smooth progression of scale when moving the circular dial up, down, left, or right. This means that when sliding a dial to control volume in the *Music* application, the audio level should move on what feels like a one-to-one scale with the interface element. A small movement in the Slider should cause a nominal change in audio volume, while a drastic shift should cause a large change in audio intensity.

Much like other iOS native interface elements, the Slider works so well and feels so real, that we lose focus of the fact that we're touching a piece of glass and not a real sliding switch. Once the user can pull their attention away from the touch screen and immerse completely on the application at hand, they'll be pulled into the experience and enjoy an application. The Slider element is a simple way to focus not on the interface, but instead on the task at hand.

There's more...

Much like the Tab Bar, the Slider opens itself up to being customized to match our interface. Here's how we can go about graphically improving our Slider.

Customize our slider

We discussed the possibility of changing the Slider bar selection color from blue to another hue that better fits our application interface, but what about the slider ball?

We can customize that using a different art image as well if we prefer, tying in a better graphic for our app. In an application I worked to design, **Battery Go! Plus**, we created a custom slider ball for a doodle theme:

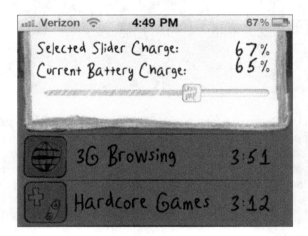

See also

▸ *Speeding up data entry through pickers* and custom keyboards in Chapter 4
▸ *Placing visual elements for touch* in the Preface

Offering complex control through an Action Sheet

What do we do when we need to temporarily allow the user to quickly select between one of three or four options, but it seems out of place to send the user to another page in order to make the choice?

Action Sheets are designed to be a quick and unobtrusive way to present the user with multiple action items in relation to the initiated task. For example, pressing the plus button near the address bar in *Safari* initiates an Action Sheet presenting the user with the option to bookmark the current web page, add the page to the home screen, or email a link of the page to a friend:

Apple has designed the **Action Sheet** element to help provide a flexible way to quickly offer the user choice when initiating a task, which will be influential in many of our applications.

Action Sheets vary a bit between the iPhone and iPad, so we'll need to take note of the differences and properly abide by the human interface guidelines when implementing the element. For this recipe, we'll discuss our options and decide if our work could benefit from an Action Sheet.

Getting ready

Action Sheets are somewhat different elements on the iPad when compared to iPhone or iPod touch devices, so we have both on hand as an example for this recipe.

How to do it...

Action Sheets are an extremely simple interface element to include in our application. When we find ourselves needing a bit of flexibility in a cramped interface, the Action Sheet will usually come to save the day.

Action Sheets are great because they essentially allow one interface element to serve multiple functions. If we find ourselves running low on space, we can attempt to group like functions together in an Action Sheet. On the iPhone and iPod touch, Action Sheets always rise up from the bottom of the screen, with the space above the sheet darkening to indicate that it is inactive and the sheet is the foremost interface object.

Under general practices and in addition to combining similar application functions together, we should also use an Action Sheet to receive user confirmation when looking to perform a destructive task. For example, if we give the user the option to delete all personal data inside of an application, we should present an Action Sheet to confirm their decision.

When initiating an Action Sheet on the iPhone, we must always include a **Cancel** button to allow the user to dismiss the view. This button should be the choice closest to the bottom of the screen, below all other Action Sheet items.

On the iPad, Action Sheets work a bit differently in the sense that they do not rise from the bottom of the screen. Instead, these sheets are placed inside of a Popover view that lies above the rest of the screen. A **Cancel** button isn't required or recommended on the iPad, as tapping outside of the Action Sheet will close the view for the user.

As noted by Apple in the Human Interface Guidelines, our Action Sheet buttons will be default silver gradient color with black text, with two important exceptions. The **Cancel** button should be the standard dark gradient with white text, making it clear to the user that this button serves a different purpose on the preceding options. A button that performs a destructive action should be red in color with white text, with this button also being the first and highest up action on the sheet. The distinctive color and placement far away from the **Cancel** button will help minimize the risk of accidental data deletion.

How it works...

Action Sheets are a fairly common interface inclusion, mostly because they're a quick way to focus the users, attention on a specific action. The user can quickly invoke a task that requires clarification or confirmation through an Action Sheet, make their choice, then dismiss the sheet, and be back in the application interface.

Action Sheets work by focusing the user's locus of attention on an important task, which the user cannot get past without making a decision or cancelling the action. This helps to ensure that while a mobile application is often used passively on the go, an important application will receive significant attention from the user. By requiring the user to focus momentarily on the task at hand, we can eliminate frustration caused by haphazardly using our application.

See also

▶ *Properly utilizing modal views* in *Chapter 3*

Using UI to keep our user inside our application

With nearly half a million apps in the App Store, users have a good deal of choice, often downloading many applications and only using them for a brief period of time.

As developers, it is our goal to keep users inside our application for as long as possible. This is increasingly important if we rely upon advertising as a revenue model, as sponsors typically pay per impression and applications with longer impressions draw greater ad revenue.

Time spent inside our application is a key metric, and a number for which designers and developers wrestle with constantly, trying to keep users engaged for a few seconds longer with each visit. In many applications, this number is absolutely vital, with advertising money tied to the number of impressions displayed along with the length of each view.

But keeping the user inside our application is tough, especially with various marketing studies asserting that uses rarely open an application more than two or three times and when they do open an app, they don't remain inside very long.

While these statistics seem disheartening, we must also remember that the name of the iOS game is volume, and a small percentage of our users will make up a majority of our app visits. An extra minute inside the app and additional function viewed could be the difference between winning over a long-term user, or being tossed aside as an app for deletion.

Regardless as to if our app is free or paid, keeping a user inside our application will provide a less frictional experience that improves satisfaction while equating into more advertisement money or application appreciation.

In this recipe, we'll look at a few methods that will help keep users inside our application for a longer period of time.

Getting ready

To prepare for this recipe, we should have a preliminary version of our application on hand, as we will be looking for ways to modify it to increase the time spent using our work.

How to do it...

To keep the user inside of the application as long as possible, here are some tips we can go about including inside our work:

1. Use a Web View to keep the user inside the app when possible.
2. Alert the user if a function will send them outside of the application.
3. If possible don't hide the status bar.
4. If we must hide the status bar, then we should provide battery information to the user.

How it works...

At the end of the day, users who enjoy our application never want to leave our application; they're just forced to because we don't offer an interface that allows them to stay inside our work.

> ▶ With point one, we may offer the opportunity to quickly allow the user to take some time to visit a web link for more information. As an example, we may be building a *Twitter* client and it's quite common for tweets to contain web links that may be of interest to the user.
>
> Likewise, we may be building an RSS reader to offer users quick, mobile formatted pages of their favorite websites. For one reason or another, a user may want to have quick access to the original webpage for the RSS feed, maybe to find contact information about a particular blogger.
>
> Thanks to the Web View, we can easily integrate a simulated *Safari* web browser inside of our application. This quick view can allow the user to visit the web page they need or visit a link, without ever leaving the application for *Safari* or another browser.

If we don't integrate a Web View interface into our application, the user will need to copy the link over to *Safari* or a similar program in order to get to the link they're interested in. This causes friction for the user, and they'll be frustrated with the process as well as less likely to use our application.

 The same technique can be used for maps, as Apple has integrated a rich API for presenting maps inside of our application. This will keep our user from needing to move out to a different application when looking for directions or to better understand a geographical area.

▸ With regards to the second point in the previous section, while we should do our best to keep users inside of our app and away from other tools like *Safari* or *Maps*, there will be situations where we will be unable to retain users. If our application offers business contact information and our user wants to make a call, there is no alternative other than using the *Phone* application.

When users must be pushed outside of our app, we should use an **Alert View** or Action Sheet to receive confirmation from to user with regards to their choice.

For example, if we offer contact information for a restaurant, a novice user may tap the location's phone number unaware that this will engage a call and send the user away from the current screen. A quick alert can give the user a second to rethink their decision, as they may wish to see restaurant hours or recommended dishes before calling to make a reservation.

▸ As we learn in the third point, the device status bar is an important strip of information for the user, offering information on wireless signal as well as the time and approximate remaining battery life.

Unless we're designing a game application where the status bar would be out of place and distracting, we should really do our best to keep the bar visible to the user at all times.

While we may not see the time or cell signal as important, our users may find this data significant if they are waiting for a call or a meeting.

If we remove this information, it becomes more likely that the user will simply close our application and leave if they need this data, sending them away from our work.

▸ Finally, if we are developing a game, an augmented reality application, or another full screen application, we should design a menu option to display the time and battery statistics.

Using official Apple iOS API, it's possible to ask the device about the current battery percentage and time, giving us the option to display this data somewhere other than the status bar.

This way, if we have to prevent our users from seeing this information, they'll still have the option to see it if need be without leaving our application.

Integrating tools such as a Web View for browsing websites, an email controller to make a quick contact, and offering access to battery information allows the user to justify remaining inside our application for as long as possible. If we make it easy for the user to work their way our app without being kicked out, they'll be more willing to explore features and see what else our product offers.

See also

> ▸ *Getting quick updates with Alert Views in Chapter 3*

Making text fade in or out of view

Scrolling bodies of text are common inside of any application; however it often looks awkward when text disappears abruptly at the end of scroll view. For a bit of graphical flare, it often can be appealing to have it appear as if the text is disappearing or fading away at the end of the screen.

In this recipe, we'll create a simple art file that will make our scrolling text appear as if it's fading away into the background.

Getting ready

For this recipe, we'll need **Photoshop** or another raster image editing program. It will also be useful to have a near final interface screenshot or knowledge of the background color we desire to use for the fade effect.

How to do it...

The text fade will require a simple semi-transparent PNG file that we'll lay above our text view. The art piece itself is fairly simple to create, but most developers are unaware of the technique. Let's take a look at how to get started:

1. Take a screenshot of our interface without the fade, or find the application's background art file, and open this in Photoshop. We'll use this as a guide for our fade image.

2. Create a new layer on top of this background, where we'll place the fade.

    This is where we'll place the fade while we prepare it for inclusion into our app. Here's an example of a scroll view in an application about flu prevention, and we'll be looking to make the last sentence or so disappear into the background.

3. Use the Marquee Tool to select a small area where we'll want to place our fade, then select the background color using the Eyedropper Tool and fill the entire selection with the Paint Bucket Tool.

4. Next, we'll create a selection so that we can create a solid color area for the transition to occur. This can vary in size depending upon our background and how drastic of a fade we desire to create.

5. Now, we should add a layer mask to the layer and use the Gradient Tool to fade the overlay from opaque to transparent.

6. This will create our fade effect. We now need to copy this layer over to its own file, save, and place the image in position above the text view in our application.

How it works...

This technique works because we're using the fade art to make it appear as if the text is slowly disappearing when in reality, it's just being covered up by a semi-transparent piece of art.

Learning layer styles and creating this piece will help us build a simple interface trick that is almost magic to the user. The text doesn't end abruptly and looks as if we've designed an advanced text management system, but all we've done is laid a simple PNG image on top of where our scroll view ends.

As we learned in steps 3 and 4, layer masks edit the transparency of our layer, so using a gradient on a layer mask will slowly transition the colored rectangle we just created from transparent to opaque. This will give the appearance that our text is fading away. Once the transparency gradient is placed upon our overlaying image, the effect will stand out as shown in the following screenshot:

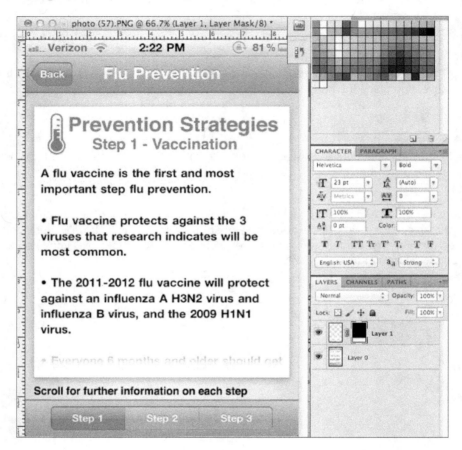

 Most users probably won't even notice this effect, but they'll subconsciously appreciate our work. The fade offers a great visual clue that more text awaits upon scrolling.

As we can see, this simple, several step technique will make our text look as if it's fading, which will offer a strong visual clue to the user that scrolling will provide more text than which is hidden away.

At this point, we only need to copy this new layer and paste it with its layer effect into a new file. From there, we can save the PNG and place it in position over the text in our application.

This is the sort of subtle and simple addition that helps make our application exceptional on the *App Store*.

There's more...

We've shown how to create a simple fade here, but what other possibilities exist for fading away text or images that scroll on screen.

Full screen? No problem

In this example, we've created a fade that does not span the entire width of the iPhone screen. However, we're not constricted by width or height in any respect with regards to creating this fade.

If we'd rather the fade out be twice as tall and the full width of the screen, that's no problem. We just need to create a piece of art that best works in our app.

High and low

It could also be likely that we would want text to fade out on the top and bottom of the scroll view. This is no problem and we can go about doing this as well. Just mirror the image, place it on the upper limit of the view, and we're good to go.

See also

▶ *Improving our application through Table Views* in *Chapter 3*

5
All About Games

In this chapter, we will cover:

- ► Planning your game around touch
- ► Control techniques that are optimized for touch
- ► Heads-up displays and designing with limited real estate
- ► Accounting for the lost Status Bar

Introduction

Games make up an exceptionally large proportion of all iOS applications, with 15 to 20 percent of all apps falling into the category. The top ten grossing applications list is consistently flooded with games, as users look for entertainment on their iPhone or iPad.

Whereas users have few expectations as to what a typical mobile application should feel like, there is often an expectation with regards to what a game should play like. Mobile gaming platforms have been popular since the Game Boy's rise to popularity in the early 90s, and users have an idea as to what games work well when on the go, and iOS games are expected to match or exceed these preconceived notions of what is possible.

However, it isn't necessarily easy to produce a game on iOS, as the device presents one of the first touch screen mobile gaming experiences. There isn't much precedent as to what game genres and control styles work well. This can be beneficial for innovation, but can also lead to a great deal of heartache for any designer.

In this chapter, we'll dive into designing a game on the iPhone or iPad, along with tips for how we can ensure a quality experience for all users on these touch screen devices. We'll discuss control techniques optimized for touch, heads up displays, and a variety of techniques to best make our game enjoyable on the iPhone or iPad.

Planning your game around touch

Unlike traditional mobile gaming platforms, we won't have physical buttons and a set interface blueprint to serve as a guide for our game.

Mobile platforms such as the **Game Boy** or **PlayStation Portable** have a physical control pad and buttons that lend the user to an inherent understanding of the game on screen. The user can quickly pick up and play a game, because they know that there is a finite set of buttons that can control game mechanics.

We're in a bit of a more difficult-to-manage scenario with iOS, as there is no control pad or face button to commonly dictate interaction on screen when in a game. Since we're on a touch screen device, we can create any interaction mechanic that we'd like, no matter how unorthodox the interface may be. This offers up an extraordinary opportunity for new gameplay experiences; however it does make our design work a bit more difficult to construct.

In this recipe, we'll discuss how touch screens drastically alter the design and playability of our game. Designing a game around touch is never an easy task. Controls are difficult to implement, screen size is often limited, and we'll need to innovate on top of standard game play mechanics to provide a fun experience.

While the operating system is only a few years old, there has been a significant evolution in gaming on the platform. Early games, such as *Super Monkey Ball* by Sega, were often ports of previous console games by big name publishers. Apple's affordable developer program allowed independent developers to step in and experiment on the platform, pushing forward intuitive new experiences like *Doodle Jump*, *Mr. AahH!!*, and *Zen Bound*. In recent years, the market has matured so that both traditional franchises and independent creative ventures can succeed.

Getting ready

To work on this recipe, it would be useful to have an iOS device along with a traditional gaming console in order to contrast the difference in mechanics between the two machines.

How to do it...

Depending on the type of game we plan on developing, there are a variety of strategies for success on the iPhone or iPad. However there are a few key attributes that will make any iOS game enjoyable:

1. Remember that users will be using the iPhone or iPad as both a screen and a controller.
2. Don't punish users for accidental interactions with the screen.
3. Keep in mind that these are mobile devices.

While a good portion of our interface will vary greatly depending upon the type of game we're looking to create, these three rules are universal and will benefit any iPhone or iPad game. With these guidelines in mind, we can move on and begin to draft up our controls and heads up display.

How it works...

The low level of entry and unique touch controls have helped iOS evolve into a platform where designers can reach outside of their comfort zone in an effort to release an innovative game on the platform.

In step one, it's important to understand that traditionally, users and designers are trained toward expecting games to have an external controller that is used for manipulation of the game world. The screen is a separate device; either a television or portable LCD screen serves as a way to project the game.

However on iOS, the screen and controller are one. Regardless as to whether users interact with our game through buttons on screen or by using a device hardware feature such as the accelerometer, it is a guarantee that the iPhone or iPad will be held in a hand while our game is being played.

We should always keep this in mind when designing both our game and interface, as the user will need to comfortably hold the device while playing. If we use traditional controls through a software joystick or buttons, we should place these elements on screen in a manner that allows for the iPhone or iPad to be held comfortably while playing. Depending upon our game and orientation, we may find that specific parts of the play area are perfect for the placement of such controls while in other scenarios, we may want to give the user the ability to customize the placement of buttons to their preference. If we expect the user to tilt or shake the controller to interact with our game, we should take this into consideration as well.

While it may sound somewhat clichéd, the game and its controls are one and the same. There is no separation and any design that assumes that we can quickly implement controls without taking this fact into consideration is destined to fail.

Not being given a set control pad or buttons gives us the flexibility to be creative, but poor design can quickly confuse or frustrate users. In the next screenshot, we can see that *Flight Control* developer Firemint has used small exclamation point markers to offer up a hint as to where inbound aircraft will soon appear. This offers a quick heads up to the user who may have had their hands in a poor position.

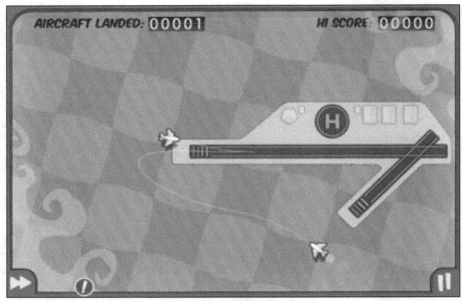

Flight Control - © 2009 Firemint Pty Inc.

We expand upon this new type of game control with these new devices in step two in the previous section. Because the game controller and device screen are so intertwined, it's very likely that the user will come into accidental contact with the screen at some point. It's just too difficult to eliminate unintended taps, as the finger is an imprecise pointing device.

We can assume that the user will make unintentional contact with the screen, and so we should do our best to design a play mechanic and interface that will not punish users for their mistake. For example, if we're building a racing game, it would be silly to place the pause button near the button used for acceleration, as misplaced fingers could often pause the game and frustrate users.

How we go about verifying this in our application can vary based on the type of game we're looking to design, but we should be mindful to keep this philosophy salient in our work. The limited ability to include a help menu in our application will encourage users to pick up app controls through point and tap experimentation. If the user experiences frustration in their first few minutes of using the app, they'll be likely to give up on using our app.

Finally in step three, we should focus on creating an interface that is mobile. While we're designing with a device that is nearly as powerful as home gaming consoles, we must keep in mind that our users will be using their iPhone or iPad when on the run. They may be playing our game on a train, or in the car, or when walking between classes, so it's important to remember that this is a slightly different game platform than what we've ever developed for before.

Because users will be playing our app when on the go and users will be less likely to sit down and play our game for extended periods of time, we should prepare our gameplay and interface around this probability.

Big buttons and forgiving controls are the best way to go about designing for a mobile interface. Larger targets on screen will make it easier for the user to perform an intended action, even when walking or riding around.

If we'd like to take mobile usability a bit further, we could also implement modifiable controls into our app as well. Giving the user the ability to calibrate settings will enable our game to play well, regardless as to the situation they're currently in. In the next screenshot, we can see how *Doodle Jump* allows users to adjust the game's controls:

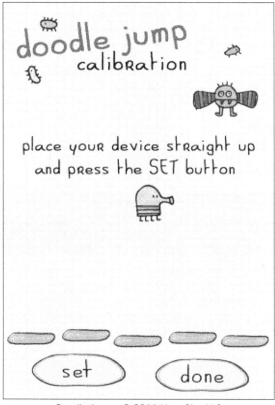

Doodle Jump - © 2011 Lima Sky, LLC

It's also important to note that we should design our interface for the rapid entry and exit that is common of iPhone users. People will be playing our game on buses, while waiting in line at a store, and in other scenarios where their time spent inside of the app may be no longer than one to two minutes. This will affect game play drastically, so it's important to test such game scenarios while we build our app.

Because our first iOS game may be our first touch screen based game, or our first game in general, we should be cautious and conservative with our interface and game play mechanics.

That's not to say that the creation of any game is easy; however these are significant pitfalls that could plague our work if we're not careful.

There's more...

While rare, there is the possibility that our iPhone can be used as a controller for a device other than itself.

Using the iPhone as a controller...for the iPad

Thanks to the **Bluetooth** integration that Apple has included in new iPhone, iPod touch, and iPad devices, it is possible to use our iPhone as a controller for iPad games, so long as the developer has produced games for both platforms and supports the feature.

It isn't necessarily easy to design and develop a game that includes such a feature, but it is by no means impossible. If we're working on an expansive game, it is definitely possible to create an immersive experience where the iPhone is used to control action on the iPad.

See also

> ▶ *Working with a finger as a pointing device in the Preface*

Using control techniques that are optimized for touch

Video games have evolved over the past 30 years to include several distinguishable and expected traits, especially with regards to controls. A joystick or control pad, and two or more physical buttons has become the standard that has seen universal success on multiple game platforms. From the original **NES** to the **Dreamcast** or **Game Boy Advance**, gamers worldwide have grown accustomed to such a scheme.

But game design drastically changes with a touch screen, as we need to properly account for how the user will hold our device, and what sort of control options will be comfortable to the user.

The fun factor of our game will be completely dependant upon the control scheme we implement into our work, so this isn't an attribute that we should take lightly. Whether we use a **software control stick**, **software buttons**, or any other interface mechanic, we should take ease of use into consideration.

For this recipe, we'll dive into different gameplay mechanics that have been proven to be successful on iOS.

Getting ready

To experience different popular control types on the iPhone and iPad, it would be useful to purchase games such as *FIFA 10* by EA Sports, *Doodle Jump* by Lima Sky, and *Ocarina* by Smule.

Both a new and old iOS device would also be useful for this exercise, so that we can experience the differences in capabilities over hardware revisions, to see how the **gyroscope** or **retina display** can alter game design.

How to do it...

Before we determine which control type is most appropriate for our game, we should first look at a few common techniques for inspiration. Here's a look at several of the options that are available for our game:

1. A traditional style using a software **simulated control stick and action buttons**.
2. Pulling, pushing, and tossing game play objects using the **flick gesture**.
3. Precise control utilizing the **accelerometer** and **gyroscope**.
4. Use of a unique hardware tool such as the **microphone** as a controller for unconventional gameplay.

In understanding the gameplay requirements for our app, we'll be better able to judge if the style of each is suitable for our work.

How it works...

The powerful processors in the iPhone, iPod touch, and iPad encourage developers to produce expansive, attractive game worlds that are equal in size and scope to traditional video games. This is great for consumers, as their new phone or MP3 player is also a first rate gaming device. However, it can create a good deal of heartache for designers.

Because such traditional gaming environments are possible, users will expect familiar controls, which is why software simulated control joysticks and action buttons are so popular in many iOS games. We can craft an experience not unlike that of a console video game, and users have rewarded those apps with strong sales in the *App Store*.

However, the lack of tactile feedback and requirement for accuracy can make such a development strategy difficult. Pair this with the intuitive hardware features of the iPhone, and many developers have gone the alternative route and created unique experiences that innovate greatly on the new platform. If original and enjoyable, these games have performed wonderfully in the store as well.

Using the simulated control stick and control button technique, we will place interface elements on screen to stand in for physical buttons. A control stick allows the user to move in any direction along an axis and buttons perform actions. We can't provide tactile feedback, but we can fake the experience enough to make it feel familiar to the user. Using this method, we can replicate any fashion of traditional controller that fits best with our game. Below, we can see how *FIFA 10* uses a traditional control style:

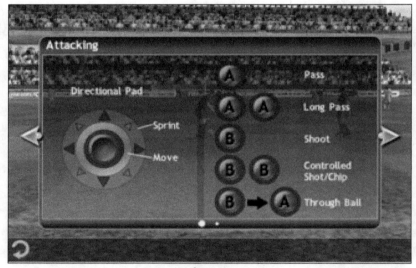

FIFA 2010 by EA SportsÔ - © 2009 Electronic Arts Inc.

Perhaps the best, and most successful example of the flick gesture gameplay mechanic is *Angry Birds*. In the game, players use a slingshot to flick tiny birds at pigs that are hiding behind a variety of barricades. The game has seen strong commercial success worldwide, mostly due to its unique controls that are only possible on a touch screen device such as the iPhone or iPad.

By requiring the users to pick up and drag birds on screen in order to determine the direction and velocity of the birds, we guarantee that the player's finger will be positioned in a place where important on screen visual cues are not obscured. Likewise, dragging a finger on screen gives a surprising amount of direct control to the user, which when coupled with a strong physics engine, provides an exceptional sense of control, as seen here:

Angry Birds - © 2011 Rovio Mobile

Doodle Jump by Lima Sky is an exceptional example of tilt controls that are powered by the accelerometer and gyroscope. As shown in the next screenshot, the user holds the iPhone or iPod touch in their hand, and then tilts left to right to help the Doodler find platforms and avoid monsters. The controls are intuitive and it feels as if the user is directly controlling a world that lives inside the iPhone, which creates an enjoyable game play mechanic.

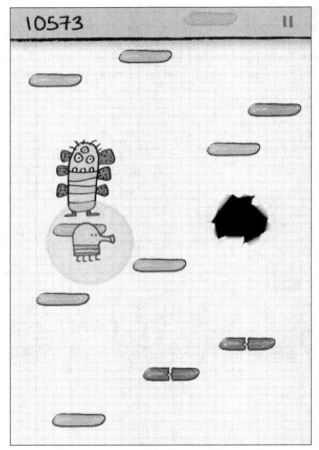

Doodle Jump - © 2011 Lima Sky, LLC

Our games can also utilize other device hardware features as well. *Ocarina* by Smule is an original experience and digital music instrument, where the user blows into the phone to play the instrument, just like a real ocarina. This is another great example of using the unique device features of iOS to create an interesting and fun entertainment option.

Picking a control type and accompanying interface is never a simple decision, and our choices will ultimately determine the success of our app in the market. The applications in this recipe should help provide inspiration and put us on the right track for application interface success.

There's more...

Users and peripheral designers have been wishing for an actual controller attachment for iOS since the *App Store's* creation, but have they found success?

Using an actual control pad

Because the iPhone and iPod touch are such powerful devices with easily accessible API for app creation, consumers have demanded an accessory that gives the devices a physical control pad for several years.

It seems as If the development of a controller shell would be easy, but such hardware attachments would need Apple's blessing in order to interact with the standard 30 pin port used on all iPhone, iPod, and iPad devices.

Thus far, Apple has never approved such an accessory, and they don't seem interested in changing their minds here in the near future. Several homebrew, small-run test controllers have been produced which would work either through Bluetooth or through jailbreaking a device, but none of these options have seen commercial success. For now, it appears as if a controller attachment will remain on iOS developer wish lists.

See also

> ▸ *Working with a finger as a pointing device in the Preface*

Designing HUDs with limited real estate

The **Heads Up Display (HUD)** is an integral aspect of any game, offering graphical overlay information on the user's score, the number of lives remaining, information on current user attributes or power ups, progress through a level, and more.

If we're designing a game, we're probably going to need a HUD. However, since our touch capacitive screen also contains our control mechanism, we need to be a bit creative with how we lay out our HUD.

In this recipe, we'll give examples of several applications that offer exceptional HUDs that we can use for inspiration in our games.

Getting ready

We don't really need any concrete hardware or software for this recipe, but we should have a good grasp of what overlay elements we'll require in our application before we begin.

We don't need to have their final shape or size set, but we should have an idea of what we'll need screen real estate for.

How to do it...

The HUD plays an important role in a game, offering up updated statistics, scoring, and important information about the user's progress in our game. As such, the HUD should flow well so that the user can quickly find this information when necessary without causing frustration. On the iPad and iPhone, this is a bit more difficult than a traditional gaming console, as we may also have game control buttons placed upon the screen as well. Here are a few tips for HUD creation:

► In designing our HUD, the first thing we should determine is what important elements are required for the user to successfully play the game.

► If we find ourselves adding seemingly too much to our HUD, we should keep in mind that it is possible to keep less essential game information on a pause screen if need be.

► Arguably the most important attribute to keep in mind when developing a HUD, is the assurance that control elements are clearly separable from non-interactive HUD content, and that our HUD never be covered by our hands while playing the game.

While we design our HUD, we will see success so long as we keep in mind the fact that the user will need to interact with the screen to play the game as well. So long as it's clear as to what on screen elements are interactive, and we place other informative on screen items in a location where it will be consistently visible and unobtrusive, users will find great utility in our HUD.

How it works...

When people think of the most important attributes of a game, they often first have controls or graphics come to mind. The HUD is often never even considered as an important attribute, even though it may be the most significant aspect of the entire design.

In reality, people don't cite the HUD as important because it's the unappreciated aspect of the system that no one really ever sees. If the HUD is good, it blends in so well and is nearly invisible so that the user can always focus on the game at hand and is never distracted by it. If the HUD is bad, users will focus their frustration on the game in general, overlooking HUD design flaws and assuming that the game itself is bad.

For the first point, we'll want to provide a HUD that offers up all the information that the user will need, while not crowding the play area. On iPhone and iPod touch devices, we're already working with a small screen area as it is, and we shouldn't over clutter our interface.

Shown in the next screenshot, *The Incident* succeeds with a minimal HUD, where important elements somewhat outline the screen. This helps to guarantee that the user can always keep attention on the game's fast paced action.

The Incident - © 2011 Big Bucket Software

With regards to the second point, we should consider moving cluttered on screen items off to a pause menu if need be. Through the pause screen or deep menu items, we can keep our game screen orderly, while offering relatively easy access to such game options. *Game Dev Story* is one such game that works well with a deep menu system.

Game Dev Story - © 2011 Kairosoft Co.,LTD

Hand placement should be the primary focus with the third point. We should make sure that buttons are clearly buttons so that users can properly hold and manage the device during gameplay. When designing an artistic vision for our buttons and background items, we should be sure to make our interface elements distinguishable and clear to the user. Seen in the next screenshot, *Chu Chu Rocket* implements a clean HUD with clearly labeled interface buttons, making the game easy to pick up and understand:

Chu Chu Rocket - © 2010 SEGA

On the surface, this makes the HUD seem like a somewhat thankless addition to our work, with no user noticing enough to appreciate the work. However, once we begin to understand the subtle traits of good HUD and their impact on a game's success, we'll realize that the entire experience is dependent on good work. By working to optimize our HUD as best we can, we'll be making the right steps toward designing a successful game.

There's more...

While developing our HUD, we may find it difficult to limit the amount of information we need on screen. We may also find it difficult to best present such options on screen. What do we do in these situations?

Customizations

If we find ourselves having difficulty, we should remember that iOS is a completely flexible design canvas. If we're unsure of what is best, we can always integrate a settings page into our application where users can make a decision on what best works for them.

This flexibility can give users a variety of options, allowing alternate interfaces for left handed users or even the ability to drag and selectively place elements if we want to work such a feature into our app.

There is no requirement that we offer such customization, however it can be a simple way to increase user satisfaction for our game.

See also

▸ *Placing visual elements for touch* in this chapter
▸ *Planning your game around touch* in this chapter

Accounting for the lost Status Bar

Because a game is typically full screen, in order to provide an immersive experience in our game, we'll lose the important 20 pixel **Status Bar** located on the top of our iPhone or iPad screen.

The Status Bar contains important user information on connectivity signal, the time, and battery life; we may not want to completely remove this functionality if we can avoid it. Users often enjoy such features and may want to know how much battery life they have or what time it is when playing our game. However, we don't want them to close our app in order to find this information.

In this recipe, we'll discuss ways in which we can best go about keeping these features inside of our application, so the user is never forced to leave midway through a game level.

Getting ready

Either the iPhone or iPad will work well in this recipe, as both will give an idea as to the significance of losing the status bar.

It also may be useful to read up on the **iOS Date and Time programming guide**, located at `https://developer.apple.com/library/ios/#documentation/Cocoa/Conceptual/DatesAndTimes/DatesAndTimes.html`.

You may also find interest in the **Battery Status sample code project**, located at `https://developer.apple.com/library/ios/#samplecode/BatteryStatus/Introduction/Intro.html`.

How to do it...

The Status Bar is an integral aspect of iOS, offering up essential information on every device. iPhone and 3G iPad devices place important signal strength information in the upper status bar, and all devices show the current time and battery level in the top bar as well.

This data is key for the user, especially information like battery life, as the user may be unwilling to continue using their iPhone to play games if the battery level is low and they need the phone to be usable and are unable to charge the device immediately.

However, problems arise as we design a full screen and immersive game application. Either we'll need every available pixel for our game, or the Status Bar will appear out of place, and we'll need to remove it from our work. But once we remove it, it will become quite clear to the user that they're unable to access this important information.

Luckily for us, Apple has offered wonderfully simple API to tie into, which will help us include the time and battery information into our game. The only problem that we must seriously deal with is the question of where we place this information.

The simple placement position is on a pause menu, however it's astonishing as to how many games and full screen applications either forget or refuse to attempt to include such data, even though it's extremely easy to implement. Two different possible inclusions of this data are:

> ▸ Integration of time and battery information into a pause menu so that the time and battery information fits into our game's art style

> ▸ Inclusion of the standard status bar into our game's pause menu

It's a minor addition, but will increase the likelihood that a user remains inside our application and creates a better experience for everyone. It's a win-win situation that helps to create an app that will ultimately receive better reviews on the *App Store*.

How it works...

The Status Bar is an iOS fixture, and the interface element that is most prevalent throughout the operating system, appearing in all but a handful of situations. It's also the least customizable interface element, as we're only able to alter a few aspects of its color.

With the bar also containing important data on device power and cell signal, users are going to need this data at some point. It's best to make sure that the user has a way to always access the information.

For the first suggested method of inclusion, we can easily create a stylized clock and battery icon to provide such information to the user:

The Incident - © 2011 Big Bucket Software

The Incident is an application that provides exceptional inclusion of time and battery data. In the previous screenshot, we can see a clock and battery indicator in the same enjoyable pixel art style that is found throughout the game. This method of inclusion is a wonderful way to retain the fun, playful styling of the game while also offering a feature that is extremely useful to the user.

If we'd rather go with the second suggestion and provide a more traditional display of information to our users, there is also nothing stopping us from throwing the standard Status Bar back into our application when action is paused as well. *Zen Bound 2* goes about replacing the Status Bar when paused, and as shown in the next screenshot, this works quite well for the user by providing a recognizable and clean presentation. This also allows for us to give the user access to the cellular signal, as we're unable to tap into signal strength using the approved API.

Zen Bound 2 Universal - © 2008 Secret Exit Ltd.

Regardless as to how we decide to include the Status Bar information, either through a playful and styled display as is seen in *The Incident* or through an implementation as seen in Zen Bound 2, this ability is extremely important to the user and we should work to include it in our interface.

Luckily, Apple has offered APIs such as the iOS Date and Time programming guide and Battery Status sample code project to help make programming this data into our application easy; we only need to go about designing ways to include it into our interface. This isn't an easy task necessarily, but with a bit of work, we can find a way to replace the Status Bar within our game.

Once users aren't forced to leave our app to see how much battery life is remaining or for the time, they'll be more comfortable playing our game for an extended period of time. This will lead to greater enjoyment, and our application will be more loved and receive higher rankings in the store.

See also

▶ *Planning your game around touch* in this chapter

6
Starting, Stopping, and Multitasking

In this chapter, we will cover:

- ▶ Starting the application with a proper `Default.png`
- ▶ Planning our application UI for a first impression
- ▶ Dealing with phone calls or text messages
- ▶ Preparing for a quit application in iOS 3
- ▶ Working with multitasking in iOS 4
- ▶ Periodical downloads and Newsstand in iOS 5
- ▶ Making accommodations for other apps that are multitasking

Introduction

We work our way through life with constant reminders of the importance of first impressions and final goodbyes. From an early age, these two circumstances are of extreme importance in our everyday lives.

Hellos and goodbyes are important in our iPhone apps as well. Providing a first impression is absolutely essential, as it will set the pace and initial user opinion about our entire application. Likewise, the user will retain a lasting impression based upon the experience we provide when they leave our app for a phone call or text message, and then return back looking to use our app again.

In this chapter, we'll discuss the finer points of application launching, closing, and multitasking. We'll discuss a few techniques that will help ensure that users enjoy their first experience, their transition back to other iOS apps, and their return to our application.

Starting the application with a proper Default.png

When an application loads for the first time, the user is presented with a variable duration of loading time. This period can change depending on the device processor or RAM, memory requirements of the application, current free memory available on the device, and any number of other variables.

Ideally, the user will only be required to sit through this period for a brief moment. However, this duration can last up to several seconds in length if we're loading an image intensive app on an older device.

Apple has designed a loading screen method that is required by each app, through the inclusion of a **PNG file** in our app bundle. In this recipe, we'll discuss two interface strategies for this loading period.

Getting ready

For this recipe, we should have a computer with **Photoshop** or another image creation tool. We should also have knowledge of the devices and orientation types that our application will support.

How to do it...

Loading times are an inherent problem with all types of software, regardless of platform. As hardware has increased in speed, these times have diminished, but they haven't become non-existent.

Apple created a simple design fix for this problem, offering up a quick and easy way to load an image during the loading period. Here are quick, simple steps in order to create an image that will display during the loading period:

1. We should start by designing up an art image measuring either 320 x 480 pixels or 320 x 460 pixels (or the equivalent Retina display double resolution size), containing the art piece which we would like the user to see during the loading screen.

2. Next, we should then save and name that file `Default.png`.

3. Finally, we should include that image in the resource bundle of our application project in XCode.

4. If we're creating a web application, we can also include the image in our HTML code so that the image is displayed when the user launches the web app. To do this, we should name our file `startup.png` and place the following code in our HTML header:

```
<link rel="apple-touch-startup-image" href="/startup.png">
```

iOS is designed to search the bundle for a PNG with this name, and then display it on load if it's available. Once we finish these steps, we have accomplished everything we need to do to have the image load on startup.

When it comes to design styles and technique on what we should include on the image, there are two different strategies that we can take:

The right way

Apple's documentation on the `Default.png` is fairly clear. According to their design documents, this image should serve as a clean visual of what the application would look like with no pre-populated data.

In essence, this provides the perception that the application has already loaded, but the user is just waiting for the data to populate. It's a subtle way to trick the user into thinking our app loads quicker than it actually does.

This trick works because it typically takes the brain about 2-4 seconds to see an image on screen, process the layout of what is before them, and then make a decision. Because the loading process for an application is relatively short, typically under three seconds, presenting an overlay of the interface as the `Default.png` loading image allows the brain to use this time to process what is about to be presented on screen.

Phone - © 2007-2011 Apple Inc.

As shown above, Phone, Messages, and Photos all load preview images with their `Default.png` displays, which offer the perception that the application loads very quickly. By preparing the user for the app during the `Default.png` load image period, the user will subconsciously perceive that our application loads faster than it actually does.

The wrong, but possibly preferable way

While we're supposed to use the loading image to prepare the user for our app, we may want this time to serve another purpose, such as a way to advertise our development team or *Twitter* account. It's an important and powerful moment for application branding, so we should feel free to use this moment as a way to build brand equity through use of a logo and appropriate styling.

There is no set rule that says we can't use the `Default.png` as an advertisement of sorts, and many applications succeed using this strategy.

We'll need to include a `Default.png` in the application package, to give our app something to display before loading has concluded. Depending on our application type and loading period, we should be able to include a screen that fits into one of these two methods with ease.

How it works...

Apple has designed iOS so that it is easy to present a loading screen to the user—we only need to create a PNG image, name it Default, and include it inside of our application bundle. The operating system will do the rest for us.

Because this predetermined method works so well, we can instead focus on optimizing the image to best fit into our application. It's important to remember that the Default image is the first thing that the user will ever see in our app, and we should take considerable care in the creation of the art. Attention to detail with such seemingly minute application attributes is what sets outstanding applications apart.

For some situations, creating an image that looks like similar to the first screen after launch will be ideal; as it will offer the perception that our application loads quicker than it actually does. This will increase user appreciation and enjoyment of our app.

In other situations, it may be desirable to go with this splash screen approach instead of the prescribed approach of faking application load. For applications where loading takes a considerable period of time, usually anything over four seconds, it is difficult to use the load to ease users into our app like Apple does with *Mail*, *Messages*, or *Phone*. The pause becomes so long that the user instead believes that the application has broken.

So in such situations, these banner loading `Default.png` images may provide a better alternative, offering up a way for the user to know that they have indeed loaded the correct application, but that it will still be several seconds before they're able to interact with the initial view.

Regardless of what method we choose, it will be necessary to include a `Default.png` in with the project. With a bit of work and consideration, we can create something that will win the hearts of our user base.

There's more...

Now that we've learned more about different styles of Default images, we can put a bit of extra effort into going the extra mile with the image as well. Here are a few tips on how to produce a great `Default.png`.

We can retina optimize our Default.png too

Like any other art piece, we can include a **Retina display** specific graphic inside our application. By adding the standard **@2x modifier** to the end of the image, iOS will know to pull this image instead when running a higher resolution device.

As the `Default.png` is the first image presented to the user, we should take extra effort to show that we're dedicated to a full retina optimized experience.

Prepare for multiple orientations

On the iPhone, we're limited to only one `Default.png` orientation requirement, as applications tend to be optimized for one orientation and we can create the Default image to account for the prominent orientation.

However, on the iPad, each application should be designed for optimal use in either orientation. This requires us to create two Default images, one for the app launching in portrait and another for if the app launches in landscape.

Apple has created an easy system for the simple creation of such different images. We only need to create the images and add a simple **–Portrait** or **–Landscape** modifier (for example, Default-Portrait.png) in order to launch the appropriate view.

See also

- *Migrating to the high-resolution Retina display* in *Chapter 1*
- *Planning our application UI for a first impression* in this chapter

Planning our application UI for a first impression

In the real world, we spend a good deal of time preparing for first impressions. We tuck our shirts in, spend time making sure our hair looks perfect, and iron our shirts so that they're wrinkle free. We do this because it's a common understanding that others will greatly have their feelings toward us determined on the basis of how we look or talk during our first meeting. If we don't impress them off the bat, they'll never be willing to warm up to us.

Mobile application development falls under the same sense of unspoken understanding. If our application isn't easy to manage or understand in the first 30 seconds, users will have no qualms over closing our work and deleting it off their device.

Are the colors attractive? Is information easy to access? Do they seem to know what the correct next step is? These are all important questions that the user will subconsciously answer during their first several minutes inside our work.

In this recipe, we'll discuss a couple of design decisions that we can make, in order to impress our users early.

Getting ready

Little is needed for this recipe. Ideally, the implementation of this recipe will take place throughout the course of development, as we fine tune along the way.

How to do it...

The `Default.png` image is the first visual that every user will see when they check out our app, but it isn't necessarily the first visual that their brain will take a good deal of time processing.

That honor will fall on our actual application, once loaded in full glory for all eyes to behold. It's a somewhat magical moment, as our work is first presented to the audience. Like the opening line of a play, first chapter of a book, the front door to a house, the first few minutes of a game, this is an important moment in the user's determination of what they think about our app.

So how do we present our application with its best foot forward? Here are a couple of simple tips, to help users quickly feel at home inside of our application:

▸ **Use simple, clean In-App icons to help signify key features**: When selecting icons to fall inside of Tab Bar cells or Navigation buttons, it's important to ensure that our icon use falls in line with expectations found in other applications. The magnifying glass represents search, a star presumes favorites or top performers, three dots represent that the tab contains multiple options, and a square with a pencil infers that the button composes a new email.

▸ **Start by giving users a push in the right direction**: Feel free to offer up a friendly push to the user from the get go. If we make the first step clear, the subsequent steps may become a bit more obvious, as shown in the following screenshot from Grades by Tapity:

Grades - © Tapity

▸ Hold back sound, flashy animation, or bright colors until the user has had the chance to settle in.

▸ Offer content early, if only a little taste of what is to come.

How it works...

Creating an intuitive application interface from the first second a user opens our app is an art, which requires that we shape our app carefully overtime. As we add new features, create new art, or conceive new ways to present data on screen, we should always be thinking about what a new user will think upon first presentation of our app.

For Step 1, Apple routinely updates the Mobile Human Interface Guidelines, `https://developer.apple.com/library/ios/#documentation/UserExperience/Conceptual/MobileHIG/Introduction/Introduction.html`, with suggestions on how to use icons that come built into the **iOS SDK**.

These guidelines account for a limited quantity of icons and uses, which makes it a bit difficult to gain a good grasp of how we should truly utilize such pieces in our app. While it would be impossible to create an exhaustive list of general shapes and their associated meaning on iOS, the best we can do is make ourselves familiar with as many apps as we possibly can in order to best understand how others have paved the road of user expectations.

In Step 2, we took a look at *Grades* by Jeremy Olsen. The application allows users to manage test scores and class grades, with an exceptional level of open-ended opportunity. No matter how complex or simple a class's grade scale may be, the application handles the data with ease.

The application makes such scalability easy for the user by using a simple contextual clue on initial launch. By offering direction on how to start tracking information for a class, the user is essentially given a tutorial without even realizing that they're being taught. There is no confusion as to what the first step is, and the user can jump right in and start keeping track of their grades.

For Step three, if we are in the mood, or feel as if it's necessary to make our application stand out through a good deal of noise, eccentric color, or excessive animation, that's perfectly fine. Each application has a different art strategy and depending on our target audience, these elements may very much make sense in our work.

However, we should be hesitant to use such vivid visuals or loud sounds during the user's introduction to our app. While the user may be in our target audience and enjoy our app otherwise, such sudden extreme sense stimulation may be off-putting.

Instead, we should slowly walk our users into the application and give them a chance to prepare for any noise or bright lights that we may throw their way. This way, the user is expecting whatever we decide to present. For example, if we offer loud noises right after the initial launch and our user is sitting in a quiet auditorium, the successive embarrassing situation may turn the user away from our application, just because we presented them with an unexpected bout of displeasure.

By working the user into our loud, colorful, flashy application, we'll be less likely to scare away potential long-term users in the first five minute of using our app.

With regards to Step 3, if our application is a content heavy application, such as a social network or application that features extensive listings of local sport scores, we may be inclined to encourage users to sign up for our service before we offer the meat and potatoes of our app. Most designers are confident that their content is so valuable, users will jump through whatever hoops necessary in order to gain access.

However, the typical user is an impatient soul, unlikely to fill out forms in order to gain access to an app's walled garden. Instead they'll download our app, see the frictional barrier in front of the content, and decide that they're not that interested.

By offering a quick glimpse, we hold some hope in convincing the user that our content is worth going through the sign up process. Service applications such as *Instagram* and *Twitter* do a great job at this, offering a handful of images or text entries before asking the user to sign up.

These quick entries give an example of the wealth of content laying behind the apparent barrier of a sign up form. Through these quick previews, the user can gain an idea as to whether they'll enjoy the service or not. By using a preview method such as this, users are able to gauge interest before the sign up, saving everyone's valuable time.

Finally, we know that every iOS device user is familiar with Apple's bundled applications, as they are the only applications that come pre-installed and as such, are the only applications that every user is likely to have used. We should look here for inspiration, as Apple offers a good deal of guidance with their work. When placing an icon on our Tab Bar, ask yourself if every user will instantly know the tabs function based on the imagery. If we have doubts, there is probably a better alternative icon.

In many respects, this recipe isn't so much a one-time action like many others found throughout this book. Instead, it's a design philosophy which we will fine tune as we create more applications for the iPhone or iPad.

There's more...

Tutorials and help menus were a somewhat taboo topic during the early days of the App Store, with Apple holding a hard stance that apps requiring such a menu were too complex for the mobile platform.

Times are changing a bit, with Apple themselves offering help menus in complex apps like *Garageband* or *iMovie*. Here's a tip on how to best offer support inside of our app.

Lend a helping hand

While most early apps were capable of success without a help menu, many new apps have become much more complex and require such a way to teach the user about app features.

If we want to provide help for our users, we have two choices. One thing we could do is create a specific help view; we could do something like provide a table of topics that the user can tap upon in order to learn more about. This allows us to dive in-depth into a variety of topics, with as much detail as we feel is required.

We could also provide a tutorial through on screen overlays, where tapping a help button presents short tips on screen with insight into different app features. This method works well because we can directly point at an interface element and tell the user what its purpose is. However, because we're overlaying such information on top of the interface, we must be brief when using this choice.

Our app may be simple and self-explanatory enough, that we won't need one of these two methods in order to provide a help menu. However, if we think that we need to lend a hand, either of these two routes would work well.

See also

▸ *Placing visual elements for touch* in the Preface

▸ *Starting an application with a proper Default.png* in this chapter

Dealing with phone calls or text messages

iOS may be capable of multitasking on newer devices, but the foundation of the operating system is still very much focused on presenting one application at a time. Even though applications can run in the background, there is still only one app visible on screen.

So what happens if the user gets a **text message** or **phone call** while in the process of using our application? It's extremely likely that a call from mom or dad is much more important than our app, even if we'd like to believe otherwise. We have to assume that at any given moment, the user could leave unexpectedly.

So how we design our interface to transition the user in and out of the application is key. If the user has spent minutes configuring our app a specific way, and that work is lost when they leave to answer a text message, they may find themselves extremely frustrated with this experience.

For this recipe, we'll discuss ways in which we can prepare for text messages, phone calls, or anything else that may pull the user away from our app.

Getting ready

For this application, you may think that we need an iPhone with an active service plan on hand in order to test entering back into an app after having left for a text or call, but we really don't. To test this behavior, we can simply press the **Home** button and return to the home screen, then re-launch our app.

When a user leaves for a text message or phone call, no special processes are going on behind the scenes, and the operating system handles the event much like any other instance in which the user quits and leaves our app. So we only need to press the **Home** button and leave in order to test this scenario.

How to do it...

So what's the best way to go about preparing our application for persistent back and forth switching? Here are a few tips:

- If the user is in the middle of an action when the call or text message comes, then find a way to bring the user back to that action

- However, if the action is time sensitive, like an action in a game, find a way to ease the user back in

- In complex situations, try to offer help or a reminder about what is going on

How it works...

Phone calls or text messages are a somewhat unique with regards to the user's experience on leaving an application, as such scenarios are always sudden and unexpected.

For the first point, regardless as to if our application is optimized for multitasking in iOS 4 or not, we should be sure to save data inside of the application as often as possible. This will allow the user to ease back into the app quickly.

For example, imagine that we're writing an application that lets a user send digital postcards to friends. In our app, the user needs to select their friend's email address, select an artistic background, and compose a message. Imagine this application if no data is saved and when the user leaves to check a quick text message, their entire postcard is deleted. This experience would become rather frustrating, as the user would need to remember this problem when using the app and hold off on answering calls or messages when composing a message.

We should help the user out with this problem by saving their content in order to offer them the opportunity to continue the card they were previously working on before they left. Save intervals will vary based on what we're building, but in general, it would be optimal to save whenever new content is created.

On the second point, we don't always want to rush and place the user back in the same position they were at before they left. If we're building a game, or some other application in which timing is important, this could be disorienting and also cause frustration.

For example, a game that requires users to avoid enemy spaceships requires a strong sense of timing as pace picks up in the game. If the user receives a phone call and must leave the app, then returns after the call, we need to ease them back into the game as their sense of timing is completely off.

Working users back into our game doesn't require an advanced interface, as we may need to only create a quick several second countdown timer before restarting game play. A simple "3, 2, 1, GO!" can help get the user ready to avoid alien invasion.

In the most advanced application, we should remember that under the circumstance of a user being pulled away from the application for a call or text message, there will be little time to prepare for being pulled from the app. The user may not have time to finish an important impending complex task, which may be difficult to jump back into.

Finally, if this scenario seems likely for our application, we need to take a step back and evaluate how our interface can be designed in order to toss the user back in without fear.

A great way to go about easing the user back in, is to save their data but start the user back a step or two behind where they were when they left. We don't want to take them far back or require them to start a complex process from scratch, but walking someone back through their last step can be an easy way to refresh the memory.

We could also go about offering a quick visual overlay reminder to give a clue as to what step is required next. If we point the user toward the next step, they'll also have a sense of direction to help lead them through our app.

In the case of a phone call, the user must make what is essentially an instantaneous choice as to if they want to leave the app and answer the call. If they choose to leave, there is no time to sit and assure that all data has been saved. As such, it's our job to ensure that when they come back, it will be as if they never even left.

If our application doesn't stand up against such a test, and it takes considerable time to jump back into our app after leaving, users will find such scenarios frustrating and find another app to use instead.

There's more...

For this recipe, we focused on text messages and phone calls, so we may be lead to believe that the iPhone is the only device where we need to worry about having the user pulled away from us. But if we're working on an iPad or iPod touch compatible app, we still have a bit to worry about.

They're not text messages, but they're close enough

As of iOS 4, Apple has decided to use an alert-based notification system. This method works extremely well given the small iPhone or iPod touch screen, with a simple blue alert view popping up on screen and allowing the user to take action. Text messages arrive in this way, so the view is extremely familiar to any iPhone user.

The same alert method is also used for **local notifications** and **push notifications** as well, which means that the entirety of this recipe is also applicable to any application that uses either notification type. While such distracts are less likely on devices that can't receive calls or texts, it is still a problem we should keep in mind.

See also

> ▸ *Getting quick updates with Alert Views* in *Chapter 3*
> ▸ *Integrating push or local notifications into our app* in *Chapter 7*

Working with multitasking in iOS 4

With the advent of iOS 4, iPhone applications could finally multitask, allowing users to quickly jump back and forth between applications. In reality, the devices aren't actually multitasking; they're instead saving the state of our application temporarily until the user returns.

However, this save state allows users to jump right back where they left off. This change has brought new user expectations, and our interfaces should respond accordingly.

In this recipe, we'll break down what users expect, and how we can deliver an exceptional multitasking experience in our app.

Getting ready

To understand multitasking, we could get by using the **iOS Simulator** built into **XCode**. We would be best off with a capable device on hand, so that we could test the features on an iPhone or iPad, but it isn't a requirement.

iPhone models 3GS and beyond, third generation iPod touch devices and beyond, and all iPad models are capable of multitasking functionality.

How to do it...

In iOS 4, Apple provided new ways for our application to multitask, which has greatly benefited the overall operating system user experience. With this new technique, users can quickly switch between applications, with no need to restart their task from the beginning just because they opened a text message.

While multitasking is helpful, it isn't multitasking in the sense that we may be familiar with. Instead of letting any app run at all times, applications can perform one of six different multitasking services to enhance their app. Here is a rundown of each service, and how they'll affect the interface of our app:

- ▶ Fast app switching
- ▶ Background audio
- ▶ Voice over IP
- ▶ Background location
- ▶ Push or local notifications
- ▶ Task finishing

Multitasking has provided a variety of new features and interface complexities in iOS, which is both good and bad for our application. If used well, we can create an exceptional new experience beyond what was previously possible. However, if we become careless, we can quickly create an interface nightmare for the user. If we work to include these tips into our app, then we'll be well on the road to multitasking success.

How it works...

The most important development change of iOS 4 was the implementation of fast app switching, as all applications could now load much more quickly for the user. This change allowed users to move from task to task with ease, which in turn created a more powerful computing experience where applications could become more in-depth and feature filled.

This ability for rapid movement was the most influential change from a design standpoint, and the most important consideration change when it comes to interface design. Pre-multitasking apps were much like movies; a dedicated start and end with the expectation that the viewer will see out the entire experience. Multitasking changed the experience to be much more like a book, specifically a dictionary or encyclopedia, where the user will instead have a dedicated beginning with the assumption that they can come back whenever necessary with little friction.

Fast app switching is the one type of multitasking that we should always include in our application, as it allows for the user to quickly jump out of the app and then return back to where they had been before leaving. While the user is gone, the app isn't actually running in the background. Instead, the app is essentially frozen in memory until the user returns, when state is restored.

For most applications, little interface work will need to be done for fast app switching, as the user will be able to jump back in right where they left off. It's a great solution for users, and for designers as well.

In applications such as games, it may be best to provide the user a countdown restart to the game after returning from a fast app switch. Games typically require quick reflexes and for the user to be prepared for action on screen, and throwing them back into the game immediately may cause frustration.

Otherwise, little work is required from an interface aspect when it comes to fast app switching.

For audio applications, such as *Music* or *Pandora*, **background audio** allows for music to play in the background while the user browses other applications.

From an interface standpoint, this has always been a point of consideration as the user has always been able to play the *Music* application while using other apps, iOS 4 just allows third party App Store applications to do the same.

The biggest problem for our interface will revolve around if we use audio cues to help aid our interface, with actions on screen leading to sound effects to verify that the action has occurred successfully. The audible swoop heard when sending a message in *Mail* is a great example of this type of sound. If we include these in our app, we should verify that our application does not interfere with background audio, or force background audio to quit playing while the user is inside of our app.

If the user is playing music from *Pandora* in the background when they load up our app, it's probably because they're rather listening to their music. We shouldn't take this as an insult. Instead, we should ensure that the user will have an exceptional experience regardless as to what audio is playing.

Voice over IP (VOIP) allows applications to use Internet calling services such as *Skype* as an alternative method for calling friends or family. Such applications were previously allowed on iOS, but the user was required to remain inside the VOIP app while on the call. Now, the user can stay on the call regardless as to which application is currently open.

If we're looking to build a VOIP application, essentially no work is required for us to handle users when outside of our app. If the user is to leave, the device status bar will double in to denote the VOIP connection, much like it occurs when the user is on a regular call.

The only interface situation that we may want to consider is the scenario that occurs when the user ends a VOIP call outside of our app, as we should design the interface to be easy to understand and manage the next time they return.

The new **background location** multitasking capabilities allows us to keep note of the user's coordinates when they are using another app. This can be useful if we are developing a GPS or location-based social networking app.

From an interface standpoint, we should design our app views so that they can quickly change in order to accommodate for the user's new location, once they hop back into our application.

For example, if we're designing a social network that allows a traveling user to identify local restaurants, a slow and clunky interface may cause background location to make our app look inaccurate and useless, especially as if it appears our location is incorrect because the app interface hasn't provided obvious enough clues to inform the user that the content on the screen is adjusting to account for the new location.

Push notifications have been a fixture since iOS 3, and **Local notifications** were introduced in iOS 4 to help provide similar functionality without need of an Internet connection.

Notifications themselves don't really affect our interface, as they're more of an intrusion on another application's interface when we implement them into our app. However, we should prepare our own interface with regards to how we'll ease users back into our app if we decide to do so with the notification.

For example, an application designed to promote animal care may send a local notification to remind users that it is time to walk their dog, thanks to a timer we've set. Our two notification options for the user may be, *Walk the Dog* or *Cancel*. If the user taps *Walk the Dog*, we may prefer to send the user back into our application, where they will make note that the dog had been walked.

We should concentrate on optimizing the view that the user arrives in on, as it will quite possibly be the only view that they see while making the note and we'll want to make the experience quick and simple for the user by making it easy to enter whatever data is required so that they can get back to what they were doing.

Task finishing in iOS 4 allows our app to finalize any process that may need to finish, without requiring the user to sit and wait for the process to end. For example, if we create a photo editing application, this service could be offered to allow the photo to be uploaded to *Facebook* or *Flickr* without requiring the user to wait to finalize the upload.

The one subtle change in our interface for this feature could be a simple note or reminder to the user that our application includes this service, as it may not be directly known to the user that the feature is supported. A user may instead assume that their upload progress would be deleted if their app was closed, driving them to stay inside our application and wait when they really don't have to.

While the metaphor may be somewhat of a stretch, we should take note of the drastic fundamental changes between the two experiences and work to optimize our work accordingly.

There's more...

Multitasking brings a multitude of great features to iOS, but it does have its disadvantages as well. Here's a look at how our multitasking app may actually upset users.

Multitasking can be frustrating

While there are many advantages to multitasking, the solution can be frustrating to certain users.

The required application close on exit of iOS 3 and earlier was often seen as a significant advantage to novice users or young children. When such users became frustrated or confused with an app, they only needed to hit the big **Home** button, and then reopen the app in order to start again from the beginning. It was a crude method, but effective at solving a problem.

iOS 4 ruined this solution, which caused a bit of frustration for those who relied upon this strategy when stuck. Upon closing and reopening, the user is brought right back to the point of difficulty, unable to escape.

If we have a hunch that our target audience could be classified as "new to the operating system", we should probably provide easy access to the home view whenever possible, to offer an escape button of sorts. This way, users can still get back to square one if something does go wrong and don't know how to navigate themselves out of the jam.

See also

▸ *Making accommodations for other apps that are multitasking* in this chapter

Periodical downloads and Newsstand in iOS 5

Apple finally included a highly desired feature in iOS 5, allowing for magazines and newspaper applications to download new issues while running in the background. This simple feature allows for users to have fresh content waiting upon launch of our app.

If we're designing a magazine, newspaper, or any other type of periodical, this will be a desirable feature and we'll need to make some small interface changes to accommodate. In this recipe, we'll take a look at what we'll need to do to help our application handle this new type of multitasking in iOS 5.

Getting ready

For this application, an iPad or iPhone device running our application will be desirable to help test the multitasking features of our app.

How to do it...

Designing an application to support background issue downloading and the interface change requirements associated with the new Newsstand feature are quite simple. In a few easy steps, our interface will be ready for Newsstand:

1. Include the UINewsstandApp key in the application's Info.plist file
2. Create the server programming backend to send the new periodical background push notification to the application
3. Integrate icon art files that will allow for the periodical cover to change as content is updated periodically
4. Design an application interface that properly notifies users of new content

After instituting these quick changes, our application will be ready to shine using Newsstand on the iPhone or iPad.

How it works...

Newsstand is an easy to integrate way to help the user enjoy the daily, weekly, or monthly content that may come along with our magazine or newspaper application for iPhone or iPad. Using the simple steps above, we'll quickly be up to speed with the new form of multitasking.

In step one, we'll make a quick Boolean addition to the `Info.plist` to help indicate that our application utilizes background downloads for periodical data. Likewise in step two, our programming team will need to follow Apple's **Newsstand Kit Framework Reference** located on the **iOS Development Center** at `http://developer.apple.com/library/ prerelease/ios/#documentation/StoreKit/Reference/NewsstandKit_ Framework/_index.html#//apple_ref/doc/uid/TP40010838`.

With step three, we'll need to provide an updated icon file to represent the updated content of our periodical. Much like a magazine cover, attractive and relevant art provides an easy way to win over reader's attention and Apple has allowed for us to quickly update our icon to reflect content updates in iOS 5. We'll include these new cover art assets to the bundle of each issue and then the updated cover will display in Newsstand.

For step four, we'll need to take a look at our application individually and determine what would be the best way to provide information inside the application on updated content. We have a lot of old tools available as well, as we can use badges on the app icon in order to also indicate to the user that a new issue is available. Inside of our app, we may want to provide an Alert View or another context sensitive feature to notify the user that content has been updated inside of our periodical.

Once we've followed these simple steps, our application will be ready for Newsstand and periodical background downloading on iOS.

There's more...

Periodical background downloads are new to iOS 5, but they're not the only way to provide background task services in iOS.

Let's multitask.

Periodicals are quite an exclusive application genre and it won't be common to work on such projects for the iPhone or iPad unless we work for a big newspaper or magazine publisher.

But we can still use multitasking inside of other applications. In iOS 4, Apple allowed developers to tie their app to specific multitasking types so that music could be played in the background, VOIP calls could be made, and more.

For a complete breakdown of different multitasking options and how they can influence our application interface design, see the previous recipe titled *Working with Multitasking in iOS 4*.

See also

▸ *Making accommodations for other apps that are multitasking* in this chapter
▸ *Working with multitasking in iOS 4* in this chapter

Making accommodations for other apps that are multitasking

In a preceding recipe, we discussed a multitude of multitasking services that were introduced to developers in iOS 4, along with several suggestions as to how we could alter our interface in order to take advantage of such features.

Nevertheless, how do we optimize our interface in order to be mindful of other applications that are currently multitasking? In this recipe, we'll discuss strategies for creating a super app experience, even when other developers are attempting to steal the glory.

Getting ready

For this recipe, we should have a multitasking device on hand if possible in order to test how our app performs while other applications are running.

It is possible to simulate the tall **status bar** inside of the iOS Simulator built into XCode, but it would be ideal to experience the change in usable resolution on an actual device.

How to do it...

Any app can take advantage of multitasking, so we should prepare for the design benefits that are possible through implementing it into our own app, along with the potential compromises required when other apps include the services as well. Here's a look at a couple of potential design problems that we should be aware of when other apps are multitasking:

▶ Fast app switching

▶ Background audio

▶ Voice over IP

Now that we've discussed both ways to benefit from multitasking, as well as ways to ensure that other applications multitasking doesn't ruin our experience, we'll be more than capable of creating an application that is flexible under any circumstance.

How it works...

Being a good multitasking steward for other apps is often an important interface consideration, as it is one of those traits that is implemented in a manner that the user will never notice such subtle differences unless we've messed it up completely. And when we do mess it up, it will be painfully obvious and ruin the app experience.

Often, the problem can be solved with a little extra spacing or other minor adjustments, so the actual implementation isn't tough. It's remembering to test for such a scenario that is the hard part; as developers often overlook such use cases when on a deadline.

Optimization for fast app switching isn't the exception as much as it is the reality with iOS development in a post iOS 4 world. Because users aren't required to finish a task in one app before finishing a task in another, we'll find that it isn't uncommon to see users swapping back and forth between two or three apps in repetition and quick succession. A power user could easily slip between an RSS reader, instant messaging client, and email in a 30 second period.

To conquer this problem, our application should be continuously saving user data in preparation for an exodus. The fast app switching service offers many services to aid this inside of our application; it's just our job to assure that our application flows properly.

There really isn't a magic formula to answer the question as to what "feels right" when it comes to application entrance and exit. It's a skill that takes time, but we'll quickly recognize the flow when we see or feel it. The goal is to eliminate interface components that cause friction or increase the amount of time that it takes to open our app and accomplish a task. When a user can quickly move back and forth with ease, we'll have mastered fast app switching.

As we discussed in the previous recipe on implementing multitasking for our own gain, the biggest difficulty for our interface will occur when we depend upon the audio inside of our application but the user is currently listening to an audio track from another application.

Ideally, we should abide by the user's clear intention to listen to the previously playing track, and never interrupt this audio when possible. We should feel free to quickly interrupt if necessary for short sound effects, but we should keep the primary audio track in control of the application that had possession of the user's headphones when they entered our app initially.

Apps that are the biggest criminals of this behavior are game applications, which look to use their own audio instead of the musical track being supplied by an app like *Music* or *Pandora*.

It's important to remember that users were listening to this song before opening our application for a reason, likely because they prefer the song to a game soundtrack. This is a personal user preference that we're never going to change, so we shouldn't attempt to force our music, even if we think it's a better choice. Instead, we should allow the user to listen to their preferred track when inside our app.

While this tip applies to Voice over IP with regards to specific device multitasking services, we will also run into this same interface problem when the user is currently on a phone call or using WiFi tethering while concurrently using our application.

When such services are used, iOS doubles the size of the status bar as a way to notify the user that a phone call or tethering service is currently taking place on the device. In the following screenshot, we can see how *Calculator* solves this problem:

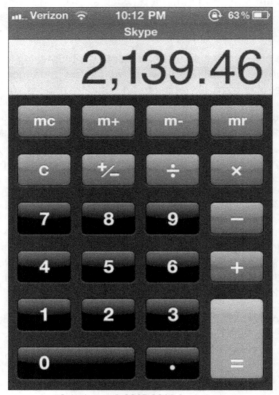

Calculator - © 2007-2011 Apple Inc.

The resulting shift gives our application essentially 20 less pixels to work with. 20 pixels only accounts for approximately four percent of our total screen height, but this distance can create a drastic shift in the appearance of our application on screen.

Depending upon how our application is coded, this double status bar will either cover up or push down part of the interface view. Such small changes seem minute, but can easyily cause a drastic difference and make parts of our application unusable.

It seems as if these situations are outliers, as an individual is less likely to be off a phone call than on a call, but these scenarios are essential because when a user enters our application when on a VOIP call or regular call, it's probably because they're looking up information to share with the person on the other line. If they are unable to access the information because of our inability to plan for the tall status bar, the user will become disappointed or frustrated with our work.

It is possible to cover the tall status bar, but only when our application is in a full screen mode where the status bar is covered throughout all use of the app. Game applications most commonly use such a behavior and while this helps eliminate the 40 pixel status bar problem, it may not be ideal for our application to always feature this trait.

The iPhone Simulator built into XCode lets us simulate these double status bar cases with ease, and we should test each view of our application for such a scenario, to guarantee that users will always be able to gather information from our app.

If we want our work to be exceptional, we should be mindful to test for the double status bar or audio problems when using our application.

There's more...

We talk a bit about the tall status bar in this recipe, but when exactly will it become a problem? Here's a look at different scenarios that can create a tall status bar.

Double status bar all the way

This 20-pixel addition to the standard status bar can cause quite a bit of design headache if we're unprepared. Here's a look at different ways in which the user can bring about the tall status bar:

  ► When on a phone call and leaving the Phone application, which is only applicable on the iPhone.

  ► When in the process of using WiFi, Bluetooth, or USB tethering, which is also only possible on the iPhone.

  ► When on a VOIP call using an application such as Skype, and the user leaves the VOIP app. This behavior is possible on all iOS devices.

  ► During an audio recording that continues to run even though the user exited the app, a double status bar will be shown. Any device with a microphone is subject to this possible double bar.

See also

  ► *Working with multitasking in iOS 4* in this chapter

7
Notifications, Locations, and Sounds

In this chapter, we will cover:

- ► Integrating push or local notifications into our app
- ► Using badges to draw attention to new content
- ► Keeping silent and managing audio properties
- ► Locating the sweet spot when handling location services
- ► Making our app useable without location data
- ► Making cents with proper ad placement

Introduction

Our application interface is not confined to the various views that take up real estate once the user is inside our application. Notifications, location management, and audio cues inside our application also take up an integral role both inside and outside of our work.

Furthermore, text clarity on messages, using badges to notify uses of content change, and location specific displays can help separate a best seller from the rest of the pack.

In this chapter, we'll discuss the inclusion of notifications, the fine sounds of background audio, location clarification, and much more.

Integrating push or local notifications into our app

Push and **local notifications** are a common inclusion in many applications, offering a way to communicate to users when they're not currently using our application. Upon a content update in our app, we can either send out a push or local notification to help allure the user back inside of our work.

Push and local notifications are an extremely useful interface option that we have essentially no creative control over. No matter how hard we try to customize the notification, it will forever be a blue rounded rectangle with one or more action buttons.

At this point, we may be asking ourselves as to if there is an actual need to put effort into the interface design of notifications. We may even wonder if time spent on such elements is even interface design work, as we have no control over the piece.

However, it's important to note that push and local notifications are often the most overlooked aspect of application design. The purpose of the notification is to encourage the user that our app is more valuable and worthwhile than whatever they're at the time of presentation.

So if we want the user to be more likely to tap through and reenter our application, we should take time to thoughtfully craft the copy and behavior of our notifications.

There isn't much interface work to be done when working to apply notifications, as a standard **Alert View** is presented with limited customization options. We do have some control over the context buttons and text included though, so we should focus on optimizing the copy and audio options that are presented when using notifications.

In this recipe, we'll dive into tips for notifications in iOS 3.0 devices and later.

Getting ready

For this recipe, we should have the knowledge regarding whether our application will use local or push notifications. We should also have advance knowledge as to what content will be presented on notifications, so that we can best prepare an optimizing text copy.

How to do it...

Here are a few helpful tips on how we can best take control of our local or push notifications:

- ▶ Consider the frequency of our expected notifications
- ▶ Be brief when displaying copy
- ▶ Provide single word, clearly identifiable action buttons
- ▶ When bringing users back into our app, create a direct route to desired content

By taking these different tips into account with our notifications, we'll create an intuitive and easily manageable way for the user to have constant communication with our application.

How it works...

Notifications are a great tool, regardless as to if we use the push or local variety. To be a success, our application requires user eyeballs, and the notification alert is a great way to remind users that they're missing out on the important content inside of our app.

With the first point on notifications, the entire element purpose is to provide the desired content to the user when outside of our application. For example, if we're creating a personal calendar application, we could send out a notification to remind the user about an upcoming event.

But we should be conservative in our decision as to how often we present such notifications, as they are somewhat disruptive when the user is viewing other content. In some respects, this disruption is appreciated, as the user has downloaded our app in order to receive such updates.

However too much of a good thing can sometimes be overwhelming, and frequent updates can become distracting and unappreciated. In determining as if we should include notifications, we should take display frequency into consideration. If we believe that we'll be presenting notifications more than once or twice per house, we may want to reconsider and look into badges instead.

Second, text presented in the body of the notification alert should be short. If we present a body copy that is longer than two to three lines in length, the alert will take considerable time to read and also runs the risk of requiring the user to scroll down through a lengthy view.

Because the push or local notification will arise when the user is busy doing something else, we should be mindful to respect their time with our interruption. Concise copy will help ensure that the user can quickly read our alert and get back to whatever they were previously occupied with.

The third tip is useful when using a two-button notification, as we're required to include the *Close* option for the user. But we are given the option to customize the action button in the notification and should take advantage of this opportunity when possible. As shown below, *Handoff* uses the word View to direct users towards new content:

If we do decide to alter the action button, a single short word is the best way to describe the task if possible. If we can't constrain the action to a single word, the button should never be so long that the text on the button is truncated and overly complex.

We should also take international language translations into consideration as well when determining the text for the action button. If our application is localized to various languages, we should verify that the text we decide upon would be printable in a concise manner in all desired languages.

Finally, when pulling the user back into our application through a notification, we should provide direct access to the updated content. Because we're interrupting the user with our notification, quick access will be appreciated.

If desirable, we are also able to include a special loading `Default.png` image to load when the user enters from a notification. This allows for a unique image that helps acclimate the user for this specific scenario. This can be done using the `alertLaunchImage` property of `UILocalNotification` class.

Many interface designers often believe that they're above worrying about the text placed on an alert, or that it's not a very influential component of the interface. This is often a significant oversight and should not be overlooked. Language is a critical component in creating clear direction, and we should persistently work to cut down on excessive or confusing copy.

Working these changes into our notifications can help drive higher tap through rates back into our application, while also offering increased user utility.

There's more...

Looking to add a bit more spunk to an alert? Here are a couple of other ways in which we can customize our notification.

Using a single button notification if we want

Throughout this recipe, we speak most specifically about two button alert notifications. However, it is also possible to create a single button alert notification too. This is useful for simple timed reminders or other content in which we're not really informing about new content, but are instead just using the alert to grab the user's attention.

Providing a positive sound

We can also include a custom sound to accompany our push or local notification. This is a great way to differentiate our alert, as the unique sound will help the user distinguish between our notification and other alert sounds for text messages or emails.

See also

▸ *Getting quick updates with Alert Views* in *Chapter 3*

▸ *Using badges to draw attention to new content* in this chapter

Using badges to draw attention to new content

As a specific form of notifications, **badges** allow us to give a numerical bit of context on the application for the user. This is a great tool when we look to inform the user on the number of their new emails, text messages, and so on.

Badges are a relatively simple, but fundamentally important aspect of an application interface. For any application that uses Push or Local Notifications in order to update the user on new content, badges are an option to help gain user attention.

Badges are used by many applications. In the previous screenshot, badges indicate the number of apps available for update in the *App Store*, emails awaiting response in Mail, replies to be viewed in *Twitter*, and more.

By definition, badges consist of a small red circle that appears in the upper right hand corner of an application or folder icon on the iOS home screen. These interface elements are technically a component in the Push and Local Notification framework, intended to be offered as an alternative to an alert notification.

When displaying a badge, we're free to offer a sound to help notify the user if we so desire. We can also display the badge in tandem with a traditional alert as well.

Badges help to offer a simple way to inform users about the number of events, messages, tasks, or other quantifiable content that is currently waiting inside of the application.

Preferably, the badge is used to offer an indication on tasks or messages that are not time sensitive. The number should indicate the number of available items that can be visited at the user's leisure, without any sense of deadline. If we feel as though our notification is for a message or task that must be completed within a specific period of time, a standard push notification is a more preferable interface option.

It's important that we use notification alerts instead of badges for time sensitive information because we can't guarantee that the user will see our badge, whereas we know they will be presented with an alert. If the user is inside of another application, on a home screen that does not include our app, or if our app is stored inside of a folder, it's very likely that the user will never see our badge.

For this recipe, we'll discuss a few badge limitations as well as the use cases that best fit the interface element.

Getting ready

To prepare for the inclusion of badges, we should ensure that our application will technically include the proper notification API. We should also have a solid understanding as to what content we will want to update users about with badges.

How to do it...

In choosing if badges are best for our application, we should consider the frequency with which we intend to present the user with information. If we feel as though our badge will often offer a number greater than 10-20 items, we may want to reconsider its inclusion. With such a large number, users will be more likely to overlook our badge and not take it seriously when our application offers up a badge display.

Badges can be updated as frequently or infrequently as we like, using Apple's notification frameworks. We can use push or local notifications to drive our badge update as we desire.

While somewhat rare, some applications use badges for other purposes. *Coaching Wizard* is an iPhone assistant for soccer coaches that provides a unique use by placing the game timer on the home screen through the use of badges. As shown below, a coach can see that the match is in the second minute when outside of the app checking e-mail or calling a player to see why they're not at the game yet:

Overall, badges are a somewhat simple, yet rather important inclusion in the interface of many feed-based applications. Graphically, they allow the user to quickly glance at an icon when on the home screen, and see the number of items currently awaiting attention.

While we're extremely limited in the presented presentation style that we're available to offer, the badge does offer a clean and simple interface opportunity for our work.

How it works...

Badges are an extremely simple interface technique that utilizes the notification framework in order to present a small red circle that indicates the number of events that haven't been acted upon. It's not highly customizable, can only be seen when the user is on a home screen and outside of our application, and offers little indication as to what is actually awaiting inside of our app.

However, the badge is an important if not overlooked way to retain user interest in our work well after they decide to leave for something else. By properly implementing this element as a way to pique curiosity, we can bring users back into our app and engage continuously. This allows the user to be informed about new app content that may interest them, while also providing our app the screen time we desire. It's win-win, and a great way to create a better app experience.

There's more...

Badges are part of the notification framework, so we can expand on them a bit. Here's a helpful tip on how to make badges stand out.

Accompanying badges with notifications

Because the badge accompanies push or local notifications in the same programming family, we can also present these alerts at the same time in which we update our badge value.

Working hand in hand, this technique can make our badge stick out more, as the user will have a more obtrusive element to overcome.

See also

▸   *Integrating push or local notifications into our app* in this chapter

Managing audio properties and keeping silent

When Steve Jobs first introduced the iPhone in 2007, he declared the device to be a phone, Internet browser, and an iPod all in one. The last point specifically was of great importance at the time, as the iPod brand was far and away the strongest line of **MP3 players** available on the market.

Immediately it became clear that the iPhone would be a pocket device designed to hold all of the user's music, movies, and more. When the *App Store* was announced, it was clear from day one that developers would be working on a platform that was used as a multi-feature device throughout the day.

As the device is most likely our user's primary audio device, we may see a situation quite often where the device is being used as an MP3 player while also using our application. As such, we should be mindful to not to hog the device's audio properties.

The most important interface function we should provide is to take note of the current audio state of the application on initial load. This is a relatively quick programming test using the **Audio Session Services framework**, specifically with the `AudioSessionGetProperty` function. By integrating this in code, we're able to queue the device and see if the audio is currently playing in the background. If there is an audio playing, it's likely that an app like *iPod* or *Pandora* is playing music that the user would prefer to listen to. As such, we should not interrupt the user's tunes and should instead find a work around.

The Audio Sessions Services serves as a valuable mechanism to help give a level of simple control for our application's audio on the device. Because audio properties can be so influential with regards to the flow of our interface, it's important to have a basic understanding of the options available to us as a designer.

Audio cues are an important aspect of exceptional interfaces, and music may be a key component in our application. But we're not always given full reign when it comes to audio inside of an application.

When the user is expecting silence, through we should respect this wish and refrain from implementing audio features that could confuse or frustrate.

In this recipe, we'll discuss the importance of respecting audio settings inside of our application.

Getting ready

For this recipe, it would be useful to understand the audio we expect to place into the application and it's purpose with regards to user experience. We'll be discussing different audio presentation options in detail, so it will be useful to understand how we intend to use sound files in app.

How to do it...

Let's take a look at the different possible audio session categories and what they mean for our application. As a note, this isn't an exhaustive list and there are several other properties available, however they are all a hybrid or minor change from the following primary categories. For an up to date and full list, we should see **Apple's Audio Session Programming Guide** located at `https://developer.apple.com/library/ios/#documentation/Audio/ Conceptual/AudioSessionProgrammingGuide/Introduction/Introduction.html`:

- ▸ **Ambient**: It is possible to make these noises interrupt the background audio track if we desire and if they are a flexible audio property. The ambient property is not designed for longer pieces though and will quit playing if the user leaves the application, which is important to keep in mind as well.

- ▸ **Playback**: We can mix in ambient noises as sound effects if desired as well as keep the playback audio playing in the background when the user leaves the app, if we feel as if it would be beneficial as well. We can also play such audio while the device is silenced as well, but should be careful of this as it may upset the user.

- ▸ **Record**: It is possible to record the audio while the device is in silent mode, and it is also possible to record the audio in the background when the user leaves our application. However, we won't be able to mix in other audio while the record property is in use.

> ► **Audio Processing**: When audio processing is running, we don't need to worry about the device and its silence settings, as no audio will be playing. As another important note, audio processing can also occur in the background on multitasking devices. So if the user leaves our app while we're still working on an audio processing job, the process will finish without the user being aware of what is going on behind the scenes.

This is a simple background into the complex world that is audio processing on the iOS platform; however it should be a good foundation for interface designers. If we understand the possibilities and expectations, we'll be able to include audio cues into our app and create a better user experience.

How it works...

Great interfaces aren't defined just by what is seen by the eyes. Audio cues and proper handling of music or sound effects are another key to strong interface design, as what happens on screen is often accompanied with audio.

Ambient noises are comparable to sound effects in video games, intended for short bursts of quick audio. These would be sounds used to help create an audio confirmation to an interface action, and are a great way to create a better application.

Playback audio would be the type of audio that you would hear when listening to a track on *iPod* or in *Pandora*. Playback is intended for long form audio such as the background music to the level of a video game.

The record property is the proper way to pick up user audio from the device microphone. This property will not work on first generation iPod touch devices, however such a device is not relatively popular at this point in time and it can be taken as a general assumption that most, if not all, of our users will have a microphone.

Audio processing is not exactly a playback possibility inside of our application, but it is an audio property nonetheless. While audio processing is occurring, the application will be using device hardware to encode audio. For example, we want to create an app that records a user's voice and then makes the user sound like a chipmunk. For an app like this, we could use background audio processing to transform the voice even if the user leaves the application. No actual sound will be heard during this period, but the device will be working behind the scenes to produce a desired file.

While we may not be designing the application's sound or programming in such code, it's important to understand what is going on inside of the application. By having a solid understanding of what opportunities are possible, as well as in knowing what makes our app's audio tick, we'll be able to better design our interface to work hand in hand with any audio track.

There's more...

While it isn't a visual attribute of the application, audio also plays an important role in creating success. Here are a few ways in which we can optimize our audio.

Audio isn't required, but it is appreciated

It's important to note that there is no Apple mandate to include audio inside our application. But it is a valuable way in which we can provide feedback to the user.

As the iPhone uses a touch screen, the device lacks buttons and it's impossible to feel with a finger when a button is pressed, which takes away any opportunity for feedback from the sense of touch. Audio can help compensate, by offering subtle sound effects to help the user confirm that they've properly interacted with our application.

Keeping those who can't hear our audio in mind too

But while audio feedback is great, we should also take user accessibility in mind, especially for potential users that are either deaf or have trouble hearing.

This means that audio cues should accompany, not substitute, our visual interface changes. This way users who can't hear the audio, or even people who have their iPhone or iPad in silent mode, can still comprehend what is happening on screen.

Locating the sweet spot when handling location services

Arguably the most powerful driver of mobile application growth has been the nearly endless idea opportunity provided through the easy accessibility to geo-location data. For the first time in computing history, it's easy and within reach to know the location of a user on the go, and then provide dynamic content on demand that is specifically tailored to that user's current position.

Location services have been one of the great benefits for application developers in the rise of the smart phone. Thanks to on-device assisted GPS capabilities; it's possible to pinpoint a user within a 10-meter radius nearly anywhere on the planet.

The ability to tap the device for location information helps us quickly grab detailed location data for use inside of the app. Because the iPhone is constantly used on the go, applications that help provide restaurant information or driving directions can be of significant value. Entering in the address or ZIP code for an unfamiliar area can be difficult, so we can instead use the device to determine the location.

Before iOS 4, it was often unclear as to when an application was obtaining location data. A simple alert prompt on initial loading of the application would ask the user to allow the use of location, but no indication was provided as to when such information was being used. Apple clarified this with the release of their new operating system, which required a special navigation icon remain in the status bar when location services were being utilized. The *Settings* application also kept note of applications that used location features, offering access to further information on the frequency of such use.

And with such further clarification, location use saw significant growth as people in general became more comfortable with the idea of their location being available at any given time to an iOS application. This is greatly beneficial for designers, as the user will typically have no problem with us grabbing their location for use. In general, so long as our application offers reward that seemingly justifies the need and we do not disobey the trust of the user, we should feel comfortable integrating location services into our app.

If we're looking to design a great interface for an application that is designed around user location, we need to take several important points into consideration. We'll be looking to provide a customized experience without overstepping any boundaries, which can be a difficult task.

In this recipe, we'll discuss **location services** and their impact on our application interface.

Getting ready

For this recipe, an iPod touch or iPad would be useful to have to hand. These devices do not have the benefit of **assisted GPS** and thus are more difficult to receive an accurate location reading on. If our application doesn't work well with the WiFi triangulation available on these devices, we'll be alienating a good deal of our user base while creating a sub-par app, so we should be sure to test on these if possible.

How to do it...

When pulling the user's location, we should always be sure to do our best to still prompt the user and pull location service data only after user action when possible. A great example of strong location use can be found in *Foursquare*. Although it is inherently understood that the app will require user location to function properly, *Foursquare* has required the user to take multiple steps when sharing their location. Here's a look at what one must do in order to share location:

1. Tap on the Friends tab.
2. Tap the **Check In** button on the Navigation Bar.
3. Select a location, which requires a manual refresh if the user has traveled a good distance.
4. Tap a large **Check In Here** button.

5. Tap another large **Check In Here** button, placed intentionally on an opposite end of the screen to ensure that the touch isn't accidental.

With such a mechanism, there is absolutely no misunderstanding between the user and application backend with regards to what is public, what is being pulled, and what the outcome will be. This is a great way to avoid negative reviews and build good will with novice users.

While the location services are useful, it is also helpful to allow the users to manually enter in their location as well. There will be times when no matter how hard we try, the GPS functionality for an individual user will not be working in our favor and there will be a desire to manually enter the data instead. If operable within our design framework, this is a significant way to increase app value.

No matter if we pull the user location automatically or through manual entry, it's important that all location centric data on screen adapt quickly to any change in location. For example, if we provide driving directions to local restaurants, we need to create our application with rapid refreshing in mind. If the user is sitting on a bus while using our app, their location could change quickly by the moment and an interface that takes an extensive period of time to update would become frustrating.

Somewhat contradictory, but also important, we must also be mindful not to pull location services too often either. This behavior may seem excessive to our users, which is definitely a problem, but it also has other unwanted side effects as well. Grabbing location from the device is one of the greatest causes of battery drain in any application and we can unnecessarily drain precious battery life.

These tips cover a fairly wide variety of different important attributes to take into consideration when integrating location services into our app. But by taking note of such subtle nuisances when dealing with location, we'll be well on our way to providing a well-rounded location aware application.

How it works...

Utilizing location data within our application is an interesting interface predicament, as we're in an awkward design period where users and developers alike are just beginning to get comfortable with understanding what is and is not acceptable with regards to user data in the mobile world.

The best advice we can take in designing our first location-aware application is to be conscious and respectful of the user's personal data. Not every person who downloads our application will be comfortable with us knowing his or her exact location, and we need to be OK with that. So instead of designing an application that punishes, we should design an app that offers flexibility and transparency.

Hopefully the tips contained in this recipe will help us build such an app. But always remember; when in doubt, err on the side of allowing the user to remain anonymous while keeping control of their personal data.

See also

▸ *Working with multitasking in iOS 4* in *Chapter 6*

▸ *Making an app usable without location data* in this chapter

Making an app usable without location data

Location services provided by the GPS, cellular tower, and WiFi triangulation methods available in iOS are wonderful inclusions in any project, allowing us to create an app where users aren't required to enter such redundant information when looking for a hotel or restaurant.

But there will be times when we can't rely on location data in our application. If our user is on an iPod touch, or on an iPhone that cannot find a tower with which to gather a GPS signal, we'll be left without a way to gather location information.

In this recipe, we'll plan out ways to optimize our location-based application when we're unable to determine where our user exactly is.

Getting ready

For this recipe, an iPod touch or Wi-Fi only iPad device would be useful to have on hand. To simulate a lack of location service data on these devices, we can simply turn WiFi connectivity off and use the application. Without this, the device will be unable to grab any data.

How to do it...

When designing an application, it's quite easy to take location data for granted. Because a majority of our users will be iPhone users, we assume that it will be simple to ask the device for coordinates and display geographically specific data on screen.

In practice, we'll find that the situation is not quite so simple, as we must also take iPod touch and WiFi iPad devices into account as well. Such devices can use **WiFi triangulation** for location data, but this requires that the user be connected to an access point which should never be taken as a given. Likewise, iPhone and iPad 3G users may find themselves with poor service and would be unable to gather coordinates.

Because accessible location data is not guaranteed, we should take this potential problem into account when designing our interface. Here are a few tips on how to optimize for such a problem:

- ▶ Allow the user to access some information without the requirement of having entered location data
- ▶ Provide clear display to the user that a device with GPS is required in order to fully utilize the application
- ▶ Give the user the opportunity to enter their location manually
- ▶ Keep track of a user's favorite location and make this information readily available

If we follow these various tips in our application, we'll be sure to provide an optimal experience, regardless as to if we have accurate data in hand. The user will find our app to be more beneficial, and we'll be rewarded with greater sales and better reviews in the *App Store*.

How it works...

While the iPhone and other smart phone devices are benefited by the addition of GPS positioning, it's a feature that can often be taken for granted. With WiFi-only iPod touch and iPad devices making up a good portion of our user base, it is important that we consider how our location-focused application will work for the user with less accurate location capabilities.

For tip 1, we see that if our application utilizes location data, we'll still want to provide some user utility without the requirement of a strong GPS signal.

We should do this because while we may not be able to provide the optimal app experience without knowing the user location, we don't want to completely turn away users from our application if they so happen to be unable to obtain their GPS coordinates. If the user is a victim of bad circumstance, they may not have the device gather an accurate location and then they'll have no possible chance for enjoyment with out app.

Instead, we should provide a preview as to what utility would be possible for the user, if GPS location was currently available. We should clearly mark such data and stress that this isn't the optimal experience, but at least the user will be able to play around and see what our application is all about. If they like what they see, they'll be willing to find a way to make GPS work and gain maximum enjoyment out of our app.

For tip 2, we shouldn't be subtle with the user in regards to a location requirement. iOS does prompt the user as to if they are willing to provide their location to our app, but we shouldn't rely on this message alone. If location is crucial for our app, we should make note of this to the user early and often.

The rationale behind this philosophy is that, we don't want the user to be taken back or surprised if our application isn't living up to their potential because we haven't received an accurate location from the iPhone or iPad. If the user is inside a large building and the device is able to obtain accurate information, then we want the user to understand that this is a result of their circumstance and not poor programming on our behalf.

By reminding the user that location is required for accurate results, and by making it clear when the device is having a hard time obtaining such data, the user will look toward blaming their situation when things go wrong, as opposed to leaving us a negative review in the *App Store*.

As we see in tip 3, when in doubt, provide a manual option for the user to enter their location. Be it through providing the city, state, or ZIP code.

Through providing this possibility for the user, we don't need to worry about the type of device or current level of user connectivity. Instead, the user can enter whatever they please, and we'll provide our data accordingly.

As shown below, the native *Weather* application provides such an option, prompting the user for their desired location to receive weather information for. Regardless as to whether the user is currently in their desired city or not, the application is able to render the optimal data.

Finally, we should also take note of user's favorite location, especially if we're developing an application where location data is pulled often. By utilizing such a method, we can help provide the most desirable location, even if our location data isn't completely accurate.

Foursquare offers such a feature as visible in the following screenshot, providing favorite check-in locations at the top of the establishment listings, even if the user is slightly outside of the typical range for that establishment. They're able to this because they know that if a user visits a certain restaurant or entertainment venue often, they're most likely going to attend again, and even if their location data is slightly inaccurate, it's likely that the user will be looking for the venue.

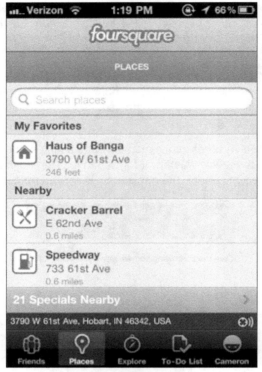

foursquare - © 2011 foursquare

Such a feature works well because it anticipates the needs of the user, and minimizes on the time spent searching it. By providing the most probable data, the user will notice that we've worked to take their personal habits into consideration, which will help grow good will for our application.

It doesn't take a good deal of work to optimize our application for such scenarios, but it does take a conscious effort. By including the tips presented in this recipe, we'll provide an experience that will be enjoyable by all, no matter what location data we are able to grab.

There's more...

If we've built a location-focused application, it isn't fun when we can't grab solid positioning information. But if we're not careful, things can head downhill very quickly.

A few apps just shutting down completely

Some applications take location to be a complete given, probably testing with only their iPhone in a big city where interesting location content is easily obtainable. When we design for something like location, we should be designing with the worst-case scenario in mind instead.

If we don't test in isolated areas and places that produce poor cell reception, we'll never have a chance to fully understand user frustration. This is increasingly apparent in location applications, where poor experiences can be exceptionally terrible and ridden with confusion or app crashing.

See also

▶   *Locating the sweet spot when handling location services* in this chapter

Making cents with proper ad placement

In the summer of 2010, Apple announced a new revenue generation tool called **iAd**. The new service was an advertisement network tailored to application developers, which partnered with strong brands in an effort to increase app profitability.

Many applications decide to insert advertisements as a way to monetize the work, so it is important that we understand the business of placing ads so that we can make informed interface decisions that help build revenue and create an immersive experience.

With regards to specific ad networks, there is a bit of variety and our options are open. This choice will be determined with the consideration of several questions, such as ease of implementation, typical revenue for our content type, fill rates, target user location, and more. The network itself will probably be chosen by our programming or marketing team, so we may not have much influence in its selection as interface designers. As such, we should be prepared to interact with anything that is thrown our way.

For the purpose of this recipe, we'll focus on iAd as it is typically the most popular and most strict with regards to interface requirement. Other ad networks tend to also be similar to iAd, so nearly all content related to the network is likely to be applicable with other networks as well.

Like any other Apple framework, the service helped simplify a process for developers while also requiring stringent standards in order to guarantee a consistent user experience. This will require that we understand the guidelines before we toss the ads into our app as well.

For this recipe, we'll discuss the various interface requirements for the iAd network, and why proper placement of such ads will increase revenue.

Getting ready

An iAd, AdMob, or other advertisement service account will be required for this exercise; however we could go about using our own self-created ad framework as well. Regardless as to what service we should decide to go with, we should have documentation on expected ad standards on hand when working through this recipe.

For more information on how to join AdMob, MobFox, or Apple's iAd networks, feel free to visit the following links:

- ▶ `http://www.admob.com`
- ▶ `http://www.mobfox.com`
- ▶ `http://advertising.apple.com/developers/`

How to do it...

While placing our ad, we're given the option of two different ad types. First is the **standard banner view**, which is available on all iOS devices. This ad type runs much like a traditional website banner ad, spanning across the width of the device screen while varying in height. For iAds, the standard banner is 50 pixels tall in portrait mode on iPhone or iPod touch and 32 pixels tall when in landscape. On iPad, the standard banner is always 66 pixels in height regardless of orientation.

The standard banner ad should always be placed on either the very bottom of the screen view, or anchored above a **Tab Bar** or **Tool Bar**, also on the bottom of the screen. Never should an iAd be placed on the top of the screen or floating in the middle of the screen. The proper placement of an iAd is shown as follows:

Battery Go! Plus - © 2011 9magnets LLC

These banners serve as an entry point to a larger ad, programmed to run full screen on top of our application when tapped.

The second advertisement type, called a **full screen banner**, is only available on the iPad. The ad type varies in height depending upon the presence of a Tab Bar or other interface item. This ad is intended to serve well as an intermittent piece between pages of a magazine or between levels of a game.

Such strong restrictions don't offer much flexibility in our interface, but offer the best opportunity to gain advertisement revenue in our app. The smaller banner ads are designed to be placed by high traffic interface items, which offer a high likelihood that the user will tap upon the ad if interest is peaked. Such banners also are designed to be as unobtrusive as possible, so that the user is never frustrated with an ad that overstays its welcome.

The **HTML 5** content rich advertisement presented once the iAd has been tapped is another exceptional way to increase the revenue, as the user is able to view a full ad without leaving the application. This makes it much more likely that the user will tap on the ad, as they won't be kicked out of whatever they are viewing in order to learn more about the featured product.

Full screen banner advertisements allow for a more traditional, large-scale marketing approach. Here, we can offer a full-page ad presentation on the iPad in-between pages of a periodical or when in a game. Such ads are immersive, well received by users, and require no sales staff in order to sell.

Using one of these advertising methods, we'll quickly create a strong application with the potential to bring in a significant amount of revenue. Just integrate the iAd framework into our existing work, and we'll be well on our way.

How it works...

For free applications, advertisement revenue can be a necessary means and important interface element. While we'd love to create amazing applications for free, income is a necessity if we're looking to make a career in app development.

Thankfully, Apple has created an exceptional ad framework along with simple and successful interface placement requirements. So as long as we sign up for the iAd program and abide by the rules, we'll be well on our way towards earning significant ad revenue from our application.

There's more...

In this recipe, we talk exclusively about the iAd platform. But we're not stuck on only one platform when it comes to placing ads inside our app.

Combining forces

Frequently, application developers integrate two or more ad platforms into an application, as one platform by itself may have a low fill rate or not be available internationally.

It's relatively easy to work two ad networks into an application from a technical standpoint, but from a design point of view, we must remember to abide by any interface standards that are required by each network involved.

The problem with this is that standards may not be consistent throughout each network. This will require us to create a fairly flexible design that works well regardless of the network.

If we do think that we're going to integrate multiple networks, it's important that we know this and plan for it up front before we get far into designing the application interface. If we design the entire app with only one network in mind, we may find it difficult to incorporate another network's interface standards late into the project cycle.

See also

 ▸ *Experiences that are possible on the iPad, but not on the iPhone in Chapter 9*

8
Accessibility, Options, and Limited Opportunity to Help our User

In this chapter, we will cover:

- ▸ Using the 80 percent rule when developing optimal settings
- ▸ Properly supporting copy and paste
- ▸ Supporting undo and redo
- ▸ Configurations in, settings out
- ▸ Cutting features when in doubt
- ▸ Supporting VoiceOver and other accessibility features

Introduction

When we're designing our application, it's extremely easy to fall into a bubble and forget that people other than our development team will use the application. It's an interesting situation, as we're mindfully creating a product for other people to use on their iPhone or iPad, but it's extremely easy to get caught up and forget that our work must be easily understandable by any user.

The most overlooked conflict arises when designers don't attempt to make their application fit into operating system wide standards such as copy and paste, undo and redo, and accessibility features such as voiceover. Often designers feel as if their app doesn't need such features, or that their app is too exceptional to require the need of accessibility features or copy and paste.

Such an arrogant designer may make such decisions because they can't look past their own experience with the app and realize that such features are implemented into the operating system to help all users feel at home inside of every application. Including such features is especially important in ensuring that disabled users are able to fully use our application, as features such as VoiceOver are essential for users who have difficulties with sight and hearing.

In this chapter, we'll discuss different ways to determine which features inside of our app should receive the most interface attention as well as ways to guarantee that we can accommodate for various system wide text properties, while also doing our best to make sure that we create an application that is usable by the disabled as well.

Using the 80 percent rule when developing optimal settings

A popular design rule, often called the **Pareto principle** in honor of the Italian economist who popularized the concept, is a fundamental theory on an **80 percent-20 percent ratio**. The basic concept behind the principle is that for a system with a large number of occurring events, often 80 percent of the results come from 20 percent of the system's cause variables.

With interface design, this rule is often embodied in the idea that for any application, 80 percent of a user's time will be spent using only 20 percent of the app's features. Many applications tend to follow this trend, with some even seeing ratios as high as 90 percent or more of all time in app spent on 20 percent of features.

In this recipe, we'll discuss how to cut down on options or features in order to best create a piece of work optimized for this principle.

Getting ready

For this recipe, it will be useful to have some sort of beta testing program planned out, so that we can get our pre-release application into the hands of users and determine what our app's most popular features are.

If we're unsure of how to best set up a beta test group, a wonderful tool awaits us at `http://www.testflightapp.com`. *Test Flight* is a simple way to distribute pre-release software to a group, and definitely worth looking into if we want to run a painless beta test.

How to do it...

As much as we would like to believe that every user would take the time to enjoy and explore every feature inside of our application, the truth is that such patterns are not typical. The 80 percent-20 percent ratio is a common standard for design guidance, with the assumption that 80 percent of all time spent inside of our application will be dedicated to 20 percent of the features inside of the application.

This means that we should bear in mind two important principles when designing our apps:

1. We should spend a good deal of time to ensure that our most commonly used app functions are easy to perform and simple to understand through the use of thoughtful interface elements.

2. We should consider the removal of less commonly used application features in an effort to focus design on essential tasks.

We may have difficulty in determining what parts of our application are most popular to a majority of users. Often, we see our applications with a bias because we played a part in their creation, and it's important to not let this personal opinion blind us to the feelings of the typical user. Because of our obvious personal preferences with regards to what is most important inside of the app, it's very important to find a metric with which to measure the application use during the beta pre-release period while we're working on the app.

 There are various analytic services for iOS development, which can help give us a peak as to what features or pages are most commonly used. Something like the **Google Analytics SDK** can be integrated quickly and offer detailed statistics as to how long the user stays inside of our app and what they do when they're visiting, which we can in turn use to determine what our most popular features are.

Likewise, we can also learn more about what features our users appreciate most through beta testing our application vigorously. This can be done by remotely offering builds via **Ad Hoc distribution**, then surveying beta testers as to what their favorite features are, or by offering test builds in person and observing the user interact with our app.

Once we have a tangible way to judge what parts of our application are most beloved by the typical user, we can go about altering our interface to better focus on the key 20 percent of features which are most commonly used. By identifying such critical components, we can make any modification necessary to help guarantee that these important features and their interface elements inside of the app are easily accessible and comprehendible by the user.

How it works...

The most important realization we can make in our interface design is that no matter how great we think each and every part of our application is, the typical user will pick out a single appealing part and focus in on that feature first and foremost.

At first, this may seem somewhat upsetting. However, we should also realize that there is nothing we can do to change the average user and instead of being discouraged, we should use such knowledge to our advantage and build a better application.

The 80 percent-20 percent rule is a great design philosophy to keep in mind when considering the idea of visual appeal. If we know that a majority of all time spent inside of our app will be focused on a small feature set, and we recognize what that feature set will be through extensive beta testing, we can use this knowledge to focus our interface around these important features. This will drive first-time users to the most significant aspects of our work, which we want them to focus on. This will help ensure attention on our best features, increasing the chance that the user will continue to use our app.

There's more...

The 80 percent-20 percent ratio is an important way to look at our app from a design perspective, but it's not exactly a set in stone rule. Here's a look at different flexibility options we have when using it.

Ratio flexibility

If we're working with users on a beta test, we don't need to fear or think our application is broken if our test users only spend 70 percent of their time on 20 percent of our app's features. Likewise, it's not overly worrisome if the user spends 90-95 percent of time on 20 percent of our features.

This tool is just a guide; don't take it too seriously when constructing your application feature set or interface.

Splitting our work into multiple apps

If we find our application full of several key features, each of which has significant value on its own, it may be best to break our application up into several different small apps.

In doing so, we may be able to offer a cleaner interface that is more feature-focused and easy to use for a specific task.

See also

▶ *Cutting features when in doubt* in this chapter

Properly supporting copy and paste

Copy and paste are two common text manipulation techniques on the iPhone and iPad, allowing users to quickly move text between fields or applications, much like on a standard desktop computer.

Copy and paste came late to iOS, not falling in place until the release of version 3.0 in the summer of 2009. Apple took their time in implementing the feature, waiting to release the functionality until they had perfected the feature interface.

In some applications, specifically iPad magazines or creative pieces with long prose, we may find it easier or more effective to take a design route that keeps the user from being able to copy and paste. Magazines are specifically notorious, displaying text content in an image so that copy and paste selection is impossible.

However, such interface behavior can be quite detrimental to the overall usefulness of our app, while also making our work much less accessible to those with disabilities. These are the outcomes that we want to prevent, so let's look at ways in which we can best utilize copy and paste in our work.

Getting ready

We won't need much for this recipe, besides a bit of knowledge as to where we anticipate the text fields being placed inside of our app.

How to do it...

By holding down a finger on a word or by double-tapping on a text area, selection cursors along with the **Edit Menu** appear on the screen so that the user can drag and select text, then copy the selection to the clipboard, as shown in the following screenshot. The user can then tap and hold or double tap on another text field to paste the text.

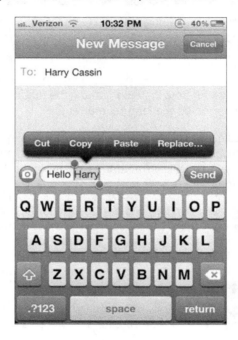

This behavior only works on text fields, through the inclusion of a menu display. Apple designed several standard menus for easy inclusion, along with the ability to customize our display as well. The only thing we need to do is have our programming team code text in the app so that it is selectable, then include copy and paste into the app.

As adding copy and paste into our application is so simple, we really need to try hard in order to keep the functionality out of our app. Some developers do in fact go out of their way to keep copy and paste from their users. Magazine publishers are often the most common example of developers that withhold copy and paste from a user. They usually refrain from including the feature or create a design where the actual app is merely a collection of JPEG images from the print edition of the magazine, and because they don't want users stealing the content.

This strategy often makes such applications much less usable, as it is impossible for the user to clip pieces and keep notes on an article or send an email to a friend with a quote from a piece. As a general practice, this is often poor because it only alienates users who look to use copy and paste, as they would expect the feature to work with any other large body of text. Disabled users who depend on VoiceOver will also be unable to use the feature with such text.

As a general practice we should always include copy and paste into our application on long bodies of text or in text fields where the user enters in their own text, and we should have a good reason to not include the selection tool if we decide to not allow the user to use such a function. Because text selection is available in so many applications, including nearly all large bodies of text, the typical user will take such a feature as given inside of our app. If we don't provide such functionality inside of our app, there will be negative feedback and it may considerably shrink the size of our potential user base.

How it works...

Copy and paste works well in iOS because the interaction is uniform throughout the operating system. If the user double taps or holds down on a text field, it's possible to select and copy or paste text.

It's important to remember though that while copy and paste is an invaluable tool that users have become accustomed to over the past two decades on the traditional desktop environment, there is little precedent on mobile phones with regards to how users initiate what they want to copy and paste, what items are selectable, and so on.

So in the design of our app, it's important to make sure we verify that the text in our work is capable of being copied if it's reasonable that the user would want to do so. Likewise, we should also be sure to let users paste text into entry fields as well.

The key to successful interface design is meeting user expectations. Copy and paste is not an extremely common tool in most applications, but we'll be setting up the user for potential frustration if we don't include the feature. That's a potential pitfall that we'd be best off avoiding. And since including copy and paste is so simple, there is really no reason not to offer this ability inside of our app.

There's more...

If we include copy and paste in our application, we'll be doing so through the Edit Menu. We can't customize much on the menu, but here are a few things we can do to give the menu a personal touch.

Menu customizations

If we want to use copy and paste, we have to play by Apple's rules and use the contextual Edit Menu. We don't have unlimited choices with regards to what we include or don't include in the menu, but here is a list of things we can do to make the menu fit into our app:

> ▶ We can choose which standard commands we want to include in the menu

> ▶ We can customize the menu's positioning, so it doesn't obscure important interface buttons

> ▶ We can choose what contents of a view are selected when the user double clicks on the screen to pull up the Edit Menu

But we can't customize everything. Here's what we don't have access to:

> ▶ The shape and sizing of the menu

> ▶ The color of the menu

See also

> ▶ *Supporting undo and redo* in this chapter

> ▶ *Supporting VoiceOver and other accessibility features* in this chapter

Supporting undo and redo

Much like copy and paste, **undo and redo** are also expected and necessary tools for easy text management on iOS. For the user looking to write a long paper on iPad or keep class notes on an iPod touch, these tools are essential.

If we want to make our app universally acceptable, including these features is a must. Over the next few pages, we'll look at the positives and negatives of including such abilities.

Getting ready

Redo and undo require little design preparation; however we should make sure that copy and paste have already been implemented into our app. These two features typically come together hand-in-hand, and if we won't be including copy and paste into our work for some specific reason, we probably won't be including redo and undo either.

Undo and redo are fairly simple text commands in any operating system, allowing for the user to quickly correct any mistakes made on screen. The functions are not as absolutely necessary as they are in a traditional computing environment, mostly because user typing will typically be in shorter and more deliberate bursts, but the ability to undo and redo is still welcome.

Apple has provided two simple and standard ways to implement undo and redo text inside of any application; we only need to implement the feature.

The first way is through the shake gesture, and this implementation can be found in the *Messages* and *Mail* application. Through a simple shake of the device, an **Alert View** slides on screen prompting the user to either undo or redo text. We can also dive further into Apple's undo and redo framework and specify which fields are capable of undo and redo, the circumstances in which the action can be preformed, and the number of levels of undo and redo which are retained. An example of undo at work after the shake gesture is as follows:

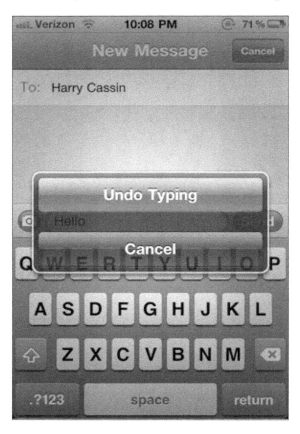

This implementation works well in applications where there is no other use throughout the application for the shake gesture, and the action will be a relatively rare occurrence. While the gesture is fairly universal system wide in typing applications as the way to undo text, we shouldn't take the action as guaranteed knowledge amongst our entire user base.

If we're building an application where we foresee undo and redo to be common functions, such as an iPad word processing application, we can always include the functions through standard buttons on a **Navigation Bar** or **Toolbar**. As shown below, *Penultimate* is a note-taking app that keeps these buttons anchored in the Navigation Bar for easy user access:

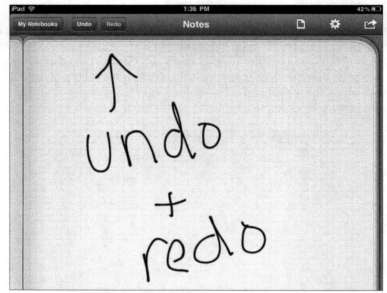

Penultimate - © 2010-2011 Cocoa Box Design LLC

Much of the undo or redo behavior will remain exactly the same if we decide to go this route instead, the actions will just be performed by tapping a button instead of shaking the device. Distinct buttons will be more apparent to the user and won't require vigorous shaking of the device, which will be greatly appreciated on the iPad especially.

Undo and redo often seem like minor features; they even stayed off Apple's feature radar until iOS version 3.0. Yet they're still important functions and we should do our best to include the set inside of our app. In designing an application worthy of a top spot in the *App Store*, consistency in presentation is key. Users will expect our app to behave like other successful apps or Apple developed applications that come standard with their device, and these works will follow the human interface guidelines and properly implement undo and redo commands.

Through working these tools into our app, we'll be one step closer to providing an experience on par with the best applications on the planet. Much like any other system feature of iOS, undo and redo won't make our application a success, but it could be a significant downfall if we happen to arrogantly overlook implementing it into our interface.

How it works...

Much like copy and paste, redo and undo are two features best included as a way to guarantee that we've met user expectations inside of our app. These two features are quite rarely used by the user, but they make our application feel more native and at home inside of iOS.

Attention to detail really stands out for the user when they determine their favorite application. With 350,000+ apps in the store, the inclusion of seemingly minor attributes such as redo and undo can really make the difference and send our application over the top and into the best sellers list.

See also

▸ *Properly supporting copy and paste* in this chapter

▸ *Supporting VoiceOver and other accessibility features* in this chapter

Configurations in, settings out

In designing iOS, Apple created a somewhat controversial and confusing design decision with regards to application settings.

iOS has been created from the ground up with the fundamental philosophy that instructional manuals and help menus are a design constraint of the past. This requires that our work be somewhat limited in feature set, in order to minimize the barrier of entry. To accommodate for this sense of minimalism, we must often limit the number of settings or configurations presentable inside of an app.

Through the developer SDK, Apple offered the ability for an app to store its configurable settings inside of the actual *Settings* application, as opposed to inside the application itself. So if the user needed to change a specific setting, they were required to leave the application, go to *Settings*, and make the appropriate change.

As one can imagine, this leads to a bit of user confusion. What's the best way to go about managing this and eliminating any potential problems? In this chapter, we'll discuss how to handle configurations and settings.

Getting ready

In preparation for this recipe, we should have a good foundation of our interface already set in place. We should also have set out exactly which options or settings we plan on presenting to our user, so that we can take this into account when deciding where to place these settings for the user.

How to do it...

To help combat confusion for novice users and save space inside of the application, Apple provided a recommended method for the presentation of app options. Through some simple coding, we can include our applications, options inside of the system's *Settings* application. On paper, this is an elegant solution that allows for developers to focus on stripping down each unnecessary piece of clutter that could keep the user's attention away from the task at hand. Below, we can see several applications that include their settings within the Settings application:

Settings - © 2007-2011 Apple Inc.

However, this solution has often lead to a great deal of user confusion as many developers keep all options inside of the application itself, leaving users unsure of where to find the proper location of the desired app setting. With no specific location for settings, either inside or outside of the application, the lost user has little direction through which to find what they're looking for.

So how do we decide on what configurations to include inside of our application and what options to place in the system *Settings* application? As a general rule of thumb, we should do our best to include commonly changed configurations inside of the application and less frequently altered options inside of the *Settings* application.

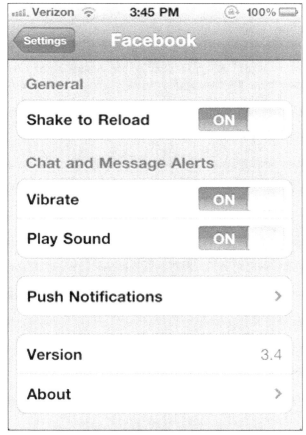

Facebook - © 2011 Facebook Inc.

A feature that is greatly dependent upon user preference, such as the frequency of sent Push Notifications, should be included inside of the application so that the user will definitely find such a setting and be able to alter it quickly. As shown above, *Facebook* is an application that follows this strategy.

Application features that are rarely altered or best left manipulated by advanced users are often best presented inside the *Settings* application. An RSS reader or *Twitter* client may want to integrate *Instapaper* support so that users can read up on articles sometime in the future. Our best interface decision may be to prompt the user for their account name and password the first time they attempt to send an article to *Instapaper*. It really won't be necessary for the user to reenter this data ever again, but should offer the opportunity to change the login credentials if need be.

The *Settings* application is also a great place to offer language customization options, as this configuration will rarely change, and *Angry Birds* is a great example of an application that takes this route. *Angry Birds* also includes another key piece of information on its *Settings* page; the application's current version number. By keeping this information outside of the app itself, it's easily obtainable if needed by support staff if the app keeps crashing.

The *Settings* page is a great place for the proper storage of information as explained in the paragraphs above. By utilizing this interface option offered by Apple, there is no need to strain and clutter our interface in order to include a way to alter something like a login credential, which will rarely if ever be used by the user.

If used correctly and the *Settings* page only includes rarely changed options, we can help simplify our in-app interface that is perfect for the novice user, while still offering the flexibility that advanced users desire.

How it works...

Apple did designers few favors with the implementation of two different ways in which to implement application settings. While this method provides us with options through which we can clean up our in-app interface, there are no specific rules with regards to what settings should be placed in the *Settings* application or inside of the application itself, which can often lead to user confusion.

In determining what settings to offer and where to place them, the "configurations in, settings out" philosophy is often a good general rule that offers the best opportunity to minimize user misunderstanding. Anything that the user may change somewhat often is best left inside of the application, with the *Settings* application housing data or options which will rarely, if ever, be needed by the user.

iOS applications rarely ever need a considerable amount of configurable options, but we must still be careful in placing the few we will have. The easier it is for the user to find what they need, the more enjoyment they will get out of our app.

There's more...

The placement of application *Settings* is a field of significant debate amongst application developers. But what if we decide we don't want to use the *Settings* application as a way to house certain options?

Do we have to?

The good news is there is nothing forcing us to include a certain amount of settings or options inside of the actual *Settings* application. If we'd prefer, we don't have to include anything there and can instead offer all options inside of the application itself.

The potential downfall with this is that our application may become a bit more complex. However, as long as we feel that this provides a better experience, there is nothing wrong with taking this route instead.

See also

- ▸ *Using the 80 percent rule when developing optimal settings* in this chapter
- ▸ *Supporting VoiceOver and other accessibility features* in this chapter

Cutting features when in doubt

If we find ourselves drowning in our own interface, unable to distinguish heads from tails, we may have a slight problem. Techniques that seem complex to us as the app's interface designer are definitely going to be too difficult to manage for the average or novice user.

Often, the cause behind clutter is the inclusion of too many features. We try too hard to make sure that we fit in every last need for every user and in doing so, we create something that no one can use properly.

Let's take a look at minimalism inside of our application design, so that we'll know when it's time to start making interface cuts for a better user experience.

Getting ready

For this recipe, we should have an understanding of what our application interface will look like. It may also be useful to have several beta testers available to offer input on user features, if we do decide something needs to be cut.

How to do it...

Let's get this bit straight upfront—the most easily avoidable mistake made in application development is the inclusion of too many features. Long feature lists are an archaic remnant of desktop applications, where we can expect a user to easily spend 30 or 40 minutes inside of the app at a time. The mobile app space is different though, and users will expect to quickly get in and use our application.

 The mobile environment almost requires that we tackle one or two tasks to perfection, offering concise instruction, and clear direction. A lack of space limits the number of interface elements that can appear on screen at any given time, so the inclusion of more than two or three tools often involves confusing menus or multiple steps.

When designing our interface, we'll often find ourselves running into a wall. In some situations, it will simply be impossible to cram in every single feature that we desire to include without creating a complicated and convoluted design. Eventually, we'll reach a point at which there will be no more space with which to include interface buttons, and that's when we'll begin to get desperate and attempt to be creative with our design work.

If we find ourselves at this junction, we should take a moment to seriously sit and contemplate the consequences of adding features to an already overloaded interface. As crazy as it may sound, when we start finding it difficult to create screen space for one feature or another, it may be best to look at features we could possibly cut instead.

While it may sound a bit counter-productive, running out of space on screen is often an early warning sign of an overdesigned interface. **Navigation Bars**, **Tab Bars**, and **Toolbars** offer more than enough space to offer simple button interactions for whatever we might need. If we find ourselves needing more, we're probably trying too hard.

iOS was designed from the ground up to be a simple operating system that performed well on the go. A need for more than a few simple tasks from any application may be asking too much, and we should hit the drawing board when we find ourselves with nowhere else to go. More likely than not, our application would be better off with fewer features if possible.

So how do we decide what should stay and what should go? The best way to go about making this tough decision is through application beta testing with a sample app audience. Friends or family work well as a test group and often offer valuable insight into what they feel is most valuable inside of the application.

Another route we can take is to perform a bit of market research on other available applications in the *App Store* in an effort to gauge what applications currently exist with a similar feature set, and where we can step in and create an application that is unique.

Once we have a grip on what features may be excessive or inessential, we can consider finding ways to decrease their prevalence in the interface, or remove them from our app completely.

Stripping down inessential features isn't a skill set, so much as it is an alternative design philosophy that has become quite prevalent as iOS and other mobile platforms have grown in market share. Traditional desktop software was often a "how much" game, while new mobile apps have become a "how quick and elegant" game instead. Complex interfaces take time to learn and have become a relic of a past computing era. If we want our iPhone or iPad app to succeed, it must be simple, intuitive, and feature focused.

How it works...

Users will be using our apps everywhere. At train stations, on bus seats, in their office, or at home; there is no guaranteed use case that we can assume will be prevalent with our app.

Desktop software developers have the luxury of knowing that a high percentage of users will be sitting on a desk and planning to use their application for an extended period of time, allowing for deep feature sets with complex interfaces. But word processors or photo editing tools don't work well while walking down the street and typing on a phone, so traditional software interfaces or features won't work well on our iOS app.

If we find our application difficult to use or overly complex, new interface elements may not solve the problem. Sometimes, we're going to need to make the tough decision and cut features from inside of our application.

It's never easy to decide what's best to cut, but hopefully we've devised a few strategies that will help us pick out what's first to go. It may seem tough to cut something that we worked so hard on, but in the end, we may be left with a better application.

There's more...

Cutting features is never a fun task, but we shouldn't toss our ideas totally by the wayside. Here's a suggestion for when to cut something.

Cut them out for now, but don't get rid of them forever

If we do decide to cut out a feature inside of our application, we should do our best to leave the function commented out in code or kept in notes somewhere so that we can refer back to the feature and possibly use it in the future.

While somewhat in contradiction to this recipe, it's important to know that there may be a time in the future where it makes sense to throw the feature back into our app. Over time, users are becoming more comfortable in a mobile computing environment and users easily understand more complex applications.

Spend a few minutes observing newer Apple created applications such as iMovie or Garageband for iPad, and compare these applications to offerings that launched with the iPhone in 2007 such as Photos, Stocks, or Weather. As users become more comfortable with an operating system, we can throw a bit more at them without fear of confusion. So while our features may not work inside of our application today, they may fit perfectly six months or a year from now. Likewise, we may also find spinning a feature that doesn't quite into an app into it's own separate app could be a successful venture as well.

See also

▶ *Using the 80 percent rule when developing optimal settings* in this chapter

Supporting VoiceOver and other accessibility features

Apple's created iOS is the most accessible mobile platform for people of all disabilities. It seems somewhat ridiculous to think that Apple could design the most intuitive smart phone for the blind, using a phone with a solid glass screen, yet they've seen significant success and become a leading manufacturer of products for the disabled due to such technologies as **VoiceOver**.

In this recipe, we'll discuss the importance of ensuring that our work will be usable by anyone, regardless of his or her physical abilities. By creating an app that can be used by the blind or deaf, we're not just enlarging our potential user base; we're also doing the right thing. Let's take a look at a few ways in which we can help guarantee that accessibility features will work inside of our app.

Getting ready

To complete this recipe, we should take some time to set up VoiceOver on our iPhone or iPad, so that we can best understand how our application works with the feature.

To enable VoiceOver, head to the **Settings** application. Under the **General** tab, **VoiceOver** can be found under **Accessibility** options.

How to do it...

When VoiceOver is implemented, the user can drag a finger across the screen and have the iPhone or iPad read the contents of the screen out loud. Once the user finds the desired content, a double tap or flick on the screen will perform a desired action.

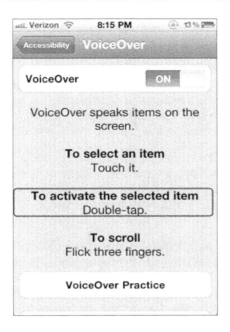

As shown above, VoiceOver requires users to interact a bit differently with iOS. Yet it's still a simple and intuitive system that requires no ability to actually see the screen. However, this ability heavily relies on the inclusion of native interface elements inside of our application.

For example, standard tools such as the Navigation Bar or Tab Bar are built from the ground up with VoiceOver in mind. If the user taps one of these buttons, the device will read out the button type and text displayed on the button. Standard icons used on these buttons are read out too, so a refresh or trash can icon will be described to the user. If a standard text view is placed on the screen, VoiceOver will read the displayed text as well.

Problems arise if we begin to design **custom interface elements**, as the speech technology will be unable to read such assets. For example, if we create a custom Navigation Bar, with the title text rendered in *Photoshop* and not in native text, the user will be unable to gain context on this text. If we create a body of text on screen but create the text in *Photoshop* in order to apply styling, then render the text in our app as an art image, this sort of element will be inaccessible through VoiceOver as well.

If we must create a unique interface element that will not contain contextual text help, it is good to know that VoiceOver will read the file names for any custom button that does not contain native text. A button containing a question mark titled **Help.png** will be read as **help**. So while we should use native attributes as frequently as possible, this method will help us make our custom features a bit more accessibility friendly.

As additional tools for aiding disabled users, Apple has created tools to allow users to zoom in on any screen or invert all colors on screen to display a higher contrast environment if so desired. Little adjustment will be needed for our interface to support such elements, although the use of native elements will be greatly beneficial with regards to zoom clarity. Native elements will be rendered at the highest resolution that Apple can include, which will look best when the user zooms in for a better view. This method will also be future proof, where if Apple does increase the resolution of a native element in a future iOS update, our interface work will also see the jump in quality for users who must view in to see.

In designing any application, it's often easy to get caught up in a design bubble, where we forget to remember that some users will not interact with or see our work as we do with our own eyes. This is especially true with regards to consideration for disabled users, and thankfully Apple has included powerful software to help make iOS a wonderful platform for all, regardless of physical ability.

As long as we implement the great tools available at our disposal, our interface will be fully capable of interacting with VoiceOver and other accessibility tools. None of the requirements for an accessible application are hard to implement; in fact in many situations, it's more difficult to not support such accessibility tools. In doing so, we'll be making our application available to a wider user base, some of whom may be experiencing mobile applications for the very first time.

How it works...

Apple has made the inclusion of accessibility features exceptionally simple. So, as long as we use standard interface elements or native text, we'll have absolutely nothing to worry about and our application will play nice with features like VoiceOver, inverted colors, zoom, and more.

In designing for the iPhone, we're working with what is arguably the greatest smart phone device ever built for the disabled, specifically for the blind. While the touch screen seems as if it would a hindrance, it provides a blank canvas through an entirely different method of interaction.

To understand the importance of designing our app for accessibility, we must first try to understand how difficult it is for a person with poor vision to use a traditional cell phone or computer. It may first seem as if such a device would be more desirable to use than a touch screen, because it would be easier to find tactile buttons to press down upon than a glass screen with no buttons. The problem with this ideology lies in the fact that the user can't see any of the buttons and as such, the device is mostly useless.

With a glass screen, there are essentially no rules by which to play by with regards to the interface. As non-disabled users, it's a fallacy to think that the iPhone is useless to the blind because we assume that they would use the device in the same manner as someone with perfect vision. In reality, the VoiceOver technology built into iOS for the disabled shows little resemblance to what the traditional user encounters and as such, it's important to handle our interface accordingly.

Working accessibility features into our app is essential because with little to no additional work, we have also created an application that is enjoyable by someone who may have never had the opportunity to enjoy a computer application like ours in the past. In a very real sense, it's our little way to make a difference and create a product that is truly special.

There's more...

We don't have to stop accommodating the disabled once we finish implementing VoiceOver. If we feel so inspired, here are a few tips to help make our app even better for the disabled.

Offering variable text size

It is quite easy to offer variable text sizes inside of our application, and we may want to consider doing so if we have a text heavy app such as an eBook reader.

While the average user may not ever have to change the size of the text inside of our app, it will be greatly appreciated by those who have difficulty in reading the text on the small screen.

Helping color-blindness too

If we have an application with a fair amount of color and art, we could have an interface that is difficult for color-blind people to read and understand.

By using colors that are high in contrast between each other, we can create something that is much more legible for the color-blind user. We can also help create a better interface for such users by not relying on colors alone to represent features or actions inside of an app.

See also

- ▶ *Using the 80 percent rule when developing optimal settings* in this chapter
- ▶ *Configurations in, settings out* in this chapter

9
Migrating to the iPad

In this chapter, we will cover:

- ▶ Migrating our app to the iPad
- ▶ Experiences that are possible on the iPad, but not on the iPhone
- ▶ Accounting for resolution and aspect ratio changes
- ▶ Managing our app for use with two hands
- ▶ Designing our app with all orientations in mind
- ▶ Including Popovers and new UI elements for the iPad
- ▶ Designing an app with skeuomorphic designs

Introduction

With the announcement of the iPad in January 2010, Apple took an emphatic leap into a market where no company had seen success before—tablet computers.

Apple was determined to prove that their entry into the field, the iPad, would stand out and succeed where others had failed. Despite initial doubt from critics, the iPad and iPad 2 have sold millions of units and become the most desirable tablet platforms for application development.

The iPad is a natural next step after working on the iPhone and iPod touch, so it's no stretch to think that we'll also be producing work on the new tablet. However, interface design does change rather drastically when moving from handheld device to tablet computer, and we should be aware of these changes when crafting a user experience.

In this chapter we'll discuss the migration to the iPad, as well as the pitfalls that lay in wait for designers creating their first work on the platform.

Migrating our app to the iPad

Upon its unveiling, the iPad was written off by critics as no more than a large iPod touch. It wasn't until the typical users were able to use the device that people soon realized that the device wasn't a magnifed version of the iPhone or iPod touch. The screen resolution, form factor, and portability of the device lent the iPad a completely different usage experience.

Let's take a look at different ways in which a user can use our app on the iPad and how this affects interface design.

Getting ready

For this application, we should have an iPad device on hand with several iPhone-only applications loaded, along with several iPad-optimized applications as well. Several well designed iPad-optimized applications to consider include Pages, GarageBand, Keynote, GoodReader, Penultimate, iMovie, and MLB.com At Bat.

How to do it...

In designing an application that we want people to use on the iPad, we're given three different types of applications that we can build, depending on if we're targeting iPhone users as well. There are three different types of applications that we can build for an iPad:

- **iPad-only application**—The application's features or interface require an iPad. This application type is impossible on the iPhone or iPod touch.

- **Universal application**—A universal application contains specific binaries for both the iPhone and iPad. Our interface will be tailored to each binary, so our application will look great regardless of platform.

- **iPhone-only application**—Designed purely for the iPhone, leaving us with only one design to create. On the iPad, our application will run through the iPhone emulator in either its native resolution or in a double resolution mode.

With these three different types of application designs, we have great flexibility with regards to the type of app we want to create. Depending upon our content or purpose, one of these styles will fit our needs.

How it works...

Apple initially created an iPhone application **emulation mode** for the iPad so that the tablet would have a library of 200,000 applications available at launch. However after using iPhone apps on the large screen, it quickly became apparent that such applications would not be an acceptable presentation for most developers. So unless we have an application that absolutely does not need an iPad version or if we are lacking the financial requirements for such a project, we should work to create an iPad optimized interface.

It's only when we begin to use an emulated iPhone application on the larger screen that we begin to understand that the iPad is not just a larger iPod touch. It becomes quite apparent that standard design tendencies on the iPhone don't always translate well when magnified up to the iPad, so we'll need to make some important decisions.

The first design decision that we need to make should be as to which application type we want to run with. Three different application types exist, each offering up a specific way in which to package and distribute our application to users. There are pros and cons for each, so we'll need to evaluate each option with regards to how it best suits our app.

Determining our audience and best application type will also depend on our development purpose, as we'll need to take programming requirements and design constraints into consideration. So long as we don't require a tablet form factor, we'll probably be targeting the iPhone with nearly every application we build as the market share. The primary question will revolve around if we decide to create a universal application or separate iPad app for the tablet.

The most common situation for which we should not consider the design of an iPad specific or **universal build** will be if our application requires telephone or text messaging functionality. If our application places on an exceptional focus on mobile use, our application may also not be worth porting to the iPad. For example, a location-centric social network like *Foursquare* doesn't necessarily require an iPad application, as it serves little use on a device larger than a phone that won't be carried around constantly.

Outside of requiring an iPhone only feature, another limiting factor in deciding to create a universal app may be extra time and cost. While the programming backend of our application remains very much the same regardless of our application type, the interface will be drastically different. When creating a universal application, we'll be designing two interfaces, one for the iPhone or iPod touch and another for the iPad. This will quickly double the amount of interface work involved and can become quite expensive if we are on a budget.

Unless our application falls into one of these two special cases, we should do our best to target iPad users with either a universal or iPad specific app. Apple has seen strong sales for the tablet and the experience of using an iPhone-only application emulated on the iPad is simply an unacceptable experience. If it makes sense for our application and we're able to, we should provide optimized versions for both iPhone and iPad users.

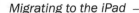

With the growing iPad market and novelty of tablet computing applications, the time spent on an iPad application will likely be well worth our time. It's a bit more difficult to create an iPad interface, especially if we've gotten in the habit of designing for the iPhone. However, the larger audience and optimal tablet experience will be sure to increase our app's fan base.

There's more...

If unable to produce an iPad-optimized application for one reason or another, we can still take an additional step to help make our work look great on the iPad.

If we can only do iPhone, we can at least increase our art quality

With the iPhone 4, Apple introduced the Retina display, for which we will likely be producing high-resolution art. But when our iPhone application is emulated on the iPad, this high-resolution art for the Retina display won't be used and our application will look somewhat blurry.

Trainyard developer Matt Rix devised an elegant solution to this problem by creating a macro that determines the device type on launch, and then displaying the Retina display art when the app is being run on the iPad.

For more information on his technique, visit Matt's blog at `http://struct.ca/2010/retinafy-your-game/`.

See also

▶ *Accounting for resolution and aspect ratio changes* in this chapter

▶ *Managing our app for use with two hands* in this chapter

Experiences that are possible on the iPad, but not on the iPhone

With the realization that the iPad wasn't a big iPod touch, it also became quickly apparent that the iPad offered up new experiences that were not initially available on the smaller devices.

Let's take a look at such new experiences, along with how our interfaces may be influenced by such potential.

Getting ready

Having an iPad on hand for testing will be useful in this recipe. Having a Macintosh on hand with a copy of *Keynote* for Mac, along with a newspaper or notepad may also be helpful.

How to do it...

The larger iPad screen has helped create a variety of new experiences that were difficult to perform or impossible on the iPhone or iPod touch. If we're unfamiliar with the iPad, it may take a bit to become accustomed to the opportunities of the new device.

Let's take a look at new genres of application experience types that have become extremely popular with the release on the iPad, and the design possibilities for these applications:

- Video-focused applications
- Desktop-style applications
- Book, magazine, and newspaper applications
- Note taking applications

These are just a few examples of application genres that have found a home on the iPad even though they had never really taken off on the iPhone and iPod touch. They're great examples of how the tablet allows for new application types, and will hopefully serve as encouragement as we work on our first designs for the device.

How it works...

The iPhone and iPad are drastically different devices, designed for different tasks and actions. Our interface design will require a bit of change as well if we plan on creating an optimized experience on iPad.

In the first year of the iPad, dozens of different new application types were created that weren't possible before on the iPhone or iPod touch. We've presented a handful here, but there are multiple other new applications along with a variety of ideas that haven't even been imagined yet.

While the iPhone has always featured a crisp widescreen display, long form video watching has never been a leading application genre on the small device, as it's often difficult to see details or focus on such a video for an extended period of time.

However, applications such as *Hulu Plus*, *Netflix*, *HBO GO*, *ABC Player*, *Crackle*, and more have created a strong video content market on the iPad. The large screen and portability makes the device great for video consumption.

If we're designing a **video-heavy app**, it's important to remember that the media is the focal point of our application. It should be easy to find desired content, start a video, control audio, send to **AirPlay**, and share favorite excerpts. It's important to remember that content is king and that the video should be the star of the show, not our interface work.

Additionally, web browsers, word processors, and remote desktop VNC applications are all different genres that have seen relatively no success on the iPhone or iPod touch, yet strong prevalence on the iPad. This has to do mostly with their "**desktop style**" presentation requirement, where it is often difficult to offer up such complex interface requirements on a small screen.

The iPad's large display gives greater interface flexibility and these applications have seen success on the device. As you can see in the next screenshot, Keynote is a technical "desktop style" application that would be difficult to implement on a screen as small as the iPhone.

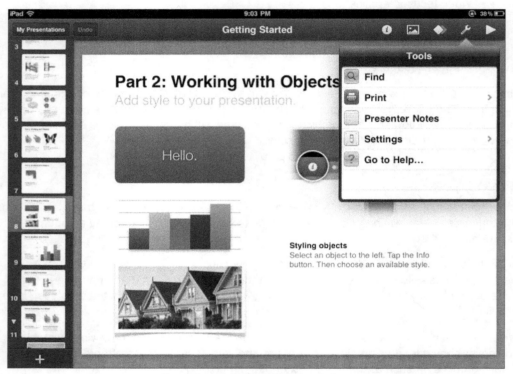

Keynote - © 2010-2011 Apple Inc.

When working on a complex application such as these, it's important to properly integrate a mix of interface elements such as a streamlined **Toolbar**, **Popovers**, and **Tab Bars** if we want to see success. The increased screen size and new elements will make it possible for such apps to work well on the iPad.

With a 9.7-inch diagonal screen, the iPad is an exceptional device for reading long form bodies of text. Reading for an extended period of time on the small iPhone or iPod touch screen can be difficult on the eyes, but the iPad screen is much like using a traditional computer. **Digital magazines**, **newspapers**, and **eBook readers** have become increasingly popular on the iPad, so it is quite likely that we could work on such an application.

When designing an application where users will be reading heavily, it's important that we focus on presenting legible text, including selectable text so that the user can copy and paste, the ability to customize font size and typeface, the addition of **AirPrint** support, easy article sharing through email or *Twitter*, and other functions which would be useful to a reader.

Finally, while it is quite rare to take notes using an iPhone or iPod touch, the iPad's large screen makes the tablet ideal for use in an educational or business setting where note taking is common. Such apps have become almost a genre of iOS applications in of themselves, with many developers jumping to get their **note-taking** app into the store.

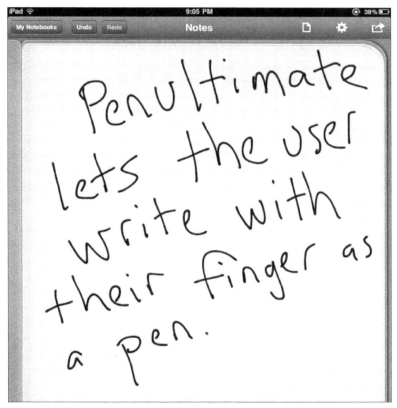

Penultimate - © 2011 Cocoa Box Design LLC

Penultimate is a successful note taking application that uses the user's finger to act as an input device on screen. In the previous screenshot, we can see an example of how handwriting looks when a finger is used to replace a pencil or pen.

If we decide to take a stab at creating our own note taking application, we'll soon realize that interface design for the app isn't a simple task. Many note applications fail because they don't make it easy to navigate through different features, making it difficult to quickly create and update notes. Likewise, apps that let the user take notes by hand often lack input accuracy, making it difficult to read what had been written. If we want our note app to stand out, ease of use and input accuracy will be key attributes for success.

These are just some of the ways in which the tablet form factor is creating waves with regards to new types of application growth. With a bit of innovation and crafty design work, we'll play an integral role in the growth of tablet applications.

There's more...

We've discussed a few software types that have become prevalent on the iPad because of the increased screen size. But what other hardware features could lead to differences between iPad and iPhone applications?

Hardware differences

Through the two iterations of the iPad, Apple has created a pattern of the iPad leading the iPhone with regards to the processor being used on the device. The first iPad received the **A4 processor** several months before the iPhone and the iPad 2 used the dual-core **A5 processor** well before the October 2011 release of the iPhone 4S.

As such, certain applications become only possible on the iPad for a period of time because they are only possible with the more powerful processor. Certain games and or intensive augmented reality apps are most likely to fit in this category.

See also

- ▶ *Accounting for resolution and aspect ratio changes* in this chapter
- ▶ *Designing our app with all orientations in mind* in this chapter
- ▶ *Including Popovers and new UI elements to the iPad* in this chapter

Accounting for resolution and aspect ratio changes

The aspect ratio of the iPad is drastically different from the iPhone. The widescreen format of the iPhone creates two drastically different formats, with the portrait view commanding a majority of application use cases and the landscape mode being relegated to mostly video consumption. In contrast, the iPad is well prepared for applications of all types in either orientation.

When working on the iPhone and iPod touch, we work strictly with a **320 pixel by 480 pixel resolution**. The iPad was introduced with a 768 pixel by 1024 pixel resolution, creating a stark screen contrast upon first announcement.

Couple this change in display with a new screen aspect ratio, moving from 1:1.5 on the iPhone to 4:3 on the iPad, and it was soon apparent to designers that such technical changes would require drastic design changes.

Let's take a look at resolution and the important role that it will play in our interface.

Getting ready

For this recipe, having a copy of *Adobe Photoshop* or another raster image manipulation tool would be useful.

How to do it...

In creating an application for iPad, we're going to have to take time to think about how the resolution change will alter our app. From a pixel pushing point of view, if we're creating a universal application and plan to share art components, we'll have a somewhat difficult time if we anticipate just throwing our Retina display art into our iPad binary. The pixel density difference is just too great and our Retina display art would look oversized and out of place if thrown into the iPad display. We'll have to go about creating new art assets that fit the new display.

Ideally, we'll create **vector** art images to use inside of our app using *Adobe Illustrator*, *Adobe Photoshop*, or another computer program. This will solve the problem forever, as we can scale our art infinitely for whatever resolution the future may toss at us. This also helps make our work flexible for future platforms as well, as we could use the same work if by chance Apple ever offers developers the opportunity to write applications for the **Apple TV** or another future device.

We'll soon learn, however, that the creation of vector art isn't easy. It requires a good eye, strong artistic talent, and knowledge of how to use a vector program. For many designers, traditional raster art is much easier to produce, so we'll be likely heading this route instead.

If we decide to create raster art in *Photoshop* or *Pixelmator*, we're going to need to make some assumptions as to what the resolution of a future Retina display iPad will look like, to use as a basis for our work:

▶ The Retina display for iPad will happen eventually; it's a matter of when, not if.

▶ The pixel density of a Retina display iPad will have a density greater than 286 PPI, which is the typically agreed upon point where the eye can no long perceive individual pixels when held 12 inches away.

- ▶ The increase in magnitude for pixels on screen for the Retina display will be a whole number, much like the iPhone's Retina display was twice as large as the original iPhone's screen. This will create an easy mathematical jump between art pieces, as non-optimized pieces will display at double their original resolution and still work just fine.

- ▶ Because the density demands of a screen three times the resolution of the original iPad is seemingly infeasible for the time being, the increased order of magnitude will probably not be larger than two.

How it works...

The change in screen aspect ratio and possibility of a drastically increased screen resolution on the iPad requires some thoughtful planning before we begin work on our application's art assets.

The 4:3 aspect ratio is a bit less optimal for video watching than the wide screen display of an iPhone or iPod touch. However, this new size allows for more width when holding the device in portrait, along with greater height when browsing applications in landscape.

With regards to resolution and the production of art assets for our application interface design, the iPad is large, but currently not a drastically different resolution than what is currently required for the iPhone. This helps during the development of universal applications, as art assets can often be easily adapted for both the iPad and iPhone.

The iPad has a native resolution of 1024 pixels by 768 pixels, a slight jump above the Retina display resolution of 960 pixels by 640 pixels. With the significant difference in pixel density between the two devices, we end up with the two drastically different devices sizes that we're presented with by Apple. In the next screenshot, we can see how the pixel scale of each screen changes as we transition from the original iPhone to the iPad.

While we're going through the effort of creating artistic elements for the iPad, we should future proof our design work and plan ahead for the eventual Retina display iPad that will inevitably come out somewhere down the line. Resolution changes are a reality of designing In pixels as opposed to paper, and we'd be poor designers if we didn't plan for the future.

Given the simple assumptions, it's highly likely that the future **Retina display iPad** will have a resolution of 2048 pixels by 1536 pixels. It's an extremely large screen size, with many experts agreeing that it would require a much faster iPad in order to process such art.

Regardless, it's nearly inevitable that we will need to produce art at this resolution eventually, so we should plan accordingly. By starting our raster artwork at this resolution, we can always easily size down for present applications, while still having Retina graphics laying in wait for the day Apple announces the Retina iPad.

Resolution independence is the primary reason it is most ideal to create application art in vectors; however these can often be difficult to produce if we're not already familiar with *Adobe Illustrator* and creating art using shapes instead of pixels. To help with this, we can make some reasonable assumptions in an attempt to estimate as to what a future Retina iPad may look like, in an effort to prepare.

It may seem unnecessary to plan in advance for a Retina display that doesn't exist yet, but we can save ourselves a great deal of pain in the future. With the release of the iPhone 4 and its Retina display, many developers were left behind with art assets that didn't easily scale up to the new screen, making their applications look dated and poor in comparison to their crisp new counterparts. By planning ahead now, we'll be able to quickly adapt and be ahead of the curve when such a device is released.

There's more...

In this recipe, we spend a good deal of time making assumptions about a future Retina display iPad. But when should we expect such a device?

When should we expect the Retina iPad?

It can be easily assumed that two factors are limiting the production of a Retina display iPad. Producing such a large screen with this resolution is probably not currently possible if Apple plans to keep their target price of $499. The device would also have a resolution that almost matches the current 27-inch desktop **Cinema Display** that Apple sells, and the processing power required to display art of such resolution would be significant.

That being said, all visible signs appear to be set toward Apple working to achieve such a device. In a rare slip, Apple's graphic design team accidentally included @2x art in version 1.2 of *iBooks* for iPad. These larger files also appear to point at a likely 2048 by 1536 pixel display as well. So if Apple's design teams are preparing for such a screen, we should probably follow suit.

Analysts first projected that such a device would not be available until 2013 and likely the iPad 4; however many hardware specialists now believe such a device could be possible for the iPad 3 in 2012. Regardless, it's only a matter of when and we should begin planning accordingly.

See also

▸ *Migrating to the high-resolution Retina display* in *Chapter 1*
▸ *Migrating our app to the iPad* in this *Chapter*

Managing our app for use with two hands

Because of the size and weight of the iPad, it becomes quite apparent that the device should naturally be held with two hands, much like a book.

Holding the device this way does create several design challenges, which will alter the way in which we drive users through our application. Let's take a look at a standard iPad interface and how to best place objects on screen so that the app is manageable while holding the device with two hands.

Getting ready

Having an iPad and iPhone on hand, along with a book or notepad for a size comparison will be helpful for this recipe.

How to do it...

The standard hand position for the iPad is different than that for the typical iPhone user, and our application must be build with this fact taken into serious consideration. The way that a device feels in the hand may have been ignored on previous computing platforms, but with the touch-based iOS, it's important that the user can hold the device comfortably while using our app correctly.

The heavier device and requirement of two hands in order to interact with the iPad will require an increase in dexterity, somewhat greater concentration, and an adjusted interface. Here are some tips to make sure that our device works well when using two hands instead of one:

▸ Increase text size for the larger screen and increased view distance
▸ Slightly increase button size for all elements
▸ Place tap buttons near the corner of the screen
▸ Use swipe and flick often; refrain from taps

The larger size and weight of the iPad will make user interaction a bit more difficult than with the traditional iPhone or iPod touch sized screen. However, when we understand the physical and physiological differences that exist between the two device types, we can adjust our interface accordingly and create a great application.

How it works...

The iPad is a larger, heavier device than its more mobile predecessors, which creates a difference in design in how we fundamentally structure our application.

While all iOS devices run the same operating system, with identical touch manipulation, the way we interact with content on screen varies quite a bit due to screen size. When we get a chance to hold both devices, it becomes easily apparent as to how each is unique.

The iPhone is typically held with only one hand, using the thumb of the same hand to quickly interact with items on screen. When typing heavily, the thumbs of both fingers may be used while holding the device in either portrait or a landscape orientation. However the iPad is much larger and heavier than the iPhone or iPod touch, making it difficult to hold the device with one hand for an extended period of time. Instead, we'll find that users traditionally hold the iPad with two hands and typical iPhone interactions are no longer possible.

We need to understand these physical limitations of the iPad, as well as the potential inconveniences that arise when using our application. We don't want to create something that requires the user to hold their iPad with one hand and tap on screen for an extended period of time, as it will become quite strenuous and users will refrain from using our app.

With regards to the first point and font size, the increase in distance from eye to screen will require a larger, more legible text for easy reading. In general, we should use a font that is at least twice as large than we would ever consider reasonable on an iPhone screen. Characters that measure one-fourth to nearly one-half an inch in physical size or larger are ideal. Font size can vary greatly based on type-face, style, and other attributes, but this should give us a good guideline to get started with.

If our application cannot be easily read while sitting two feet or slightly further away from the user's face, it will be difficult for our application to be read for extended periods of time.

Likewise, we should also slightly increase the size of our buttons on screen in order to account for the greater distance between face and device. While the minimum optimum button size for an iPhone application is a 44 pixel square, we should make our iPad buttons a minimum of 60 pixels in length or width if possible.

This increase in size also helps the users, as less hand-eye coordination is needed in order to accurately tap the proper location on screen. While user fingers will remain an average size of 44 pixels, the extra bit of leeway will give a bit more room for error.

We should consider the placement of such buttons as well when composing our interface design. On traditional mouse and keyboard computer interfaces, designers are often taught to observe **Fitts' law**, which in part explains that integral interface items should be placed close to the corners of the screen because these regions are easier for the user to quickly navigate to because the pointer will catch on the end of the screen. It's a useful observance and commonplace in good design.

Much in the same way, we should also place our iPad interface items near the corner of the screen. While we won't be using a mouse and don't need the corners to catch our pointer, such a design is cognitively simple to the user and quick to pick up. It will also allow for the user to tap on screen and not have the large display covered with their hands, giving full visibility of whatever is being altered by an action. Finally, the user's fingers will often be near the side of the screen anyway while sitting on the bezel to hold the device, so it will make for a much more rapid movement when they finally do decide to touch elements on screen.

With regards to the last point, when we do decide to require user action on screen, it's much more preferable to use swipes or flicks than it is to use taps. When possible, we should try our best to replace taps with another gesture.

Because of hand placement on the iPad, it's easier to slide over the thumb and quickly flick on screen than it is to raise a hand off of the device and tap. For nearly all users, no readjustment of the holding hand is necessary to reach with the thumb and make a swipe in any direction.

iBooks is a wonderful example of this, as the thumb can quickly swipe to change pages while the holding hand remains in place. *iBooks* also lets a user navigate from page to page by tapping the entire right side and left side of the book view. By giving a large tap zone, the user doesn't need to place their hands in any position other than what feels natural, and then make contact through a swipe or touch of the side of the screen in order to turn to the next page.

We'll gain a better understanding as to what gestures and device holding positions are more desirable as we use our gain experience using an iPad. As Apple continues to refine and adjust the device's design, it's guaranteed that the iPad will only become lighter and easier to use. But for the time being, such factors must be taken into account when attempting to build success.

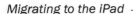

There's more...

We've discussed how the iPad will be held during use of our application, but with the growing market for iPad cases, does it make sense to design our application around the likelihood of the user having an iPad case?

Case considerations

In the year that the device has been on the market, an unbelievable number of iPad cases have been designed that attempt to help people protect their tablets.

But each case is slightly a different size, is made out of a different material, and ultimately will change the way in which the user holds the iPad.

We're better off not worrying about different case designs and their influence on our app, as we'll always find a case design that will drastically require us to change a part of our app. However if we do put energy into testing our iPad app with a case, we should only worry about Apple designed official cases. The portfolio case of the first iPad and **Smart Cover** for the iPad 2 account for an estimated 60 to 70 percent of case sales and are going to be the most common case for our user base.

See also

  ▶ *Accounting for resolution and aspect ratio changes* in this chapter
  ▶ *Designing our app with all orientations in mind* in this chapter

Designing our app with all orientations in mind

The iPhone and iPod touch are primarily portrait orientation devices, with no requirement for us to support the landscape orientation. The iPad is different and Apple states clearly stated in its **Human Interface Guidelines** that all applications should support both orientations unless there is explicit reason not to. But a 4:3 aspect ratio screen doesn't exactly make it easy to design an interface that works well in all orientations.

In this recipe, we'll discuss a few cheats that will help make it easy to design an interface that looks great in both portrait and landscape.

Getting ready

An iPad loaded with an email account in the *Mail* application and the *USA Today* application will be good to have on hand for this recipe.

How to do it...

We're given a bit of creative freedom with regards to designing an interface that is functional in either perspective. But if we're having difficulty, there are two tried and true practices that help create expedite interface development:

- ▶ The Split View method
- ▶ The Multi-pane method

With the Split View and multi-pane layout, we have some guidance as to how we can create a simple yet effective iPad app that works well in both orientations. Each method provides an attractive application and allows for us to offer a deep experience with little headache.

How it works...

While iPhone applications typically only work in one orientation, Apple thoughtfully designed the iPad to be a device with no up or down. There's no wrong way to hold an iPad and as such, there should be no wrong way to hold our application.

Such a requirement can be a daunting realization for some developers and designers, as it immediately requires that our application essentially be two applications in one.

The **Split View** is a new interface view to the iPad, which can be flexible depending on orientation. This allows us to create dynamic content that works great no matter the user's preferred device position.

When in landscape mode, the application has two distinct views separated by a black line. The left view is primarily served as a navigation menu, offering up different bits of information. The right view is typically much larger and content focused, determined by navigating through options on the left view.

When in portrait view, the Split View can take one of two appearances. If we so desire, we can keep a split view, with each different side of the screen becoming a bit narrower. If we feel cramped, we can instead create one single view and use a Popover from a Navigation Bar button to display what previously appeared on the smaller panel. *Mail* is a great example of this, offering a split view to optimize screen in both orientations. In the landscape perspective, emails appear on right and different mailbox options appear on in the left panel. When in portrait, e-mails appear in a full screen view and a Popover allows users to navigate through menu options. In the next screenshot, we can see how orientation affects *Mail*'s split pane view:

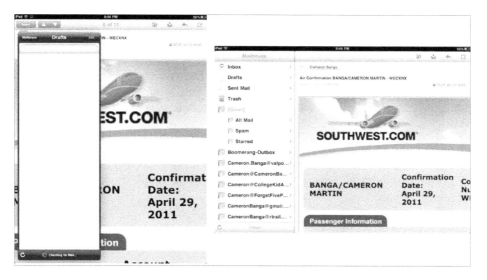

The **multi-pane method** is not unlike a Split View, in that different data appears in different sections of the interface. While the Split View focuses primarily on two views with one containing very linear data through a Navigation View, a multi-pane application can feature any number of small view pieces.

The idea of a multi-pane view is that data or app action buttons are chunked together into fixed height and width pieces. The idea being that when the user rotates the application from portrait to landscape, these fixed size chunks simply move into a new position while retaining their size. Working much like a jigsaw puzzle with multiple solutions, this method allows for applications that look unique in both orientations.

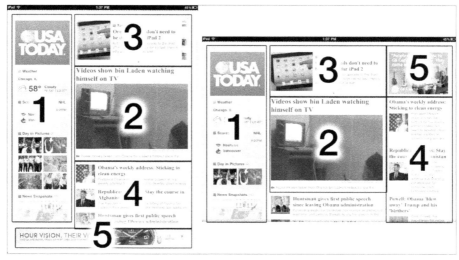

USA TODAY for iPad - © 2011 USA TODAY

As notated above, we can see the shift in content when the *USA Today* application moves from portrait to landscape. These distinct chunks of content allow for easy movement between perspectives.

Complete symmetry between perspectives isn't a complete requirement. As we can see here, the advertisement panel and a news panel change slightly when the rotation occurs. However, each individual component does have a constant presence.

The flexible multi-pane technique allows for us to quickly support both portrait and landscape views in a way that appears consistent. While the *USA Today* application contains many panes, we can use this technique with as few as two pieces. So long as we remain consistent, the user will be able to easily manage our app no matter the orientation, and we'll be able to expedite the design process.

There's more...

Looking for another example of a multi-pane view? Here's another great app that uses a similar technique.

Another example

Flipboard is a socially aggregated news application, where stories linked to by friends on *Facebook* or *Twitter* are placed on screen for consumption. It's a novel app idea and has created a large following of iPad users.

Flipboard - © 2010 Flipboard Inc.

Flipboard also uses this multi-pane design, with stories flowing on screen from portrait to landscape in set dimension boxes. If we're looking for a further example, *Flipboard* is a great place to start.

See also

▶   *Including Popovers and new UI elements for the iPad* in this chapter

Including Popovers and new UI elements for the iPad

For the larger screen, Apple has designed a series of new interface elements for the tablet device. Most of these new conventions are impossible on the iPhone or iPod touch due to screen size, so we'll be restrained in how we can use them.

Because they're relatively rarer for us, we should take time to study up and guarantee that we're using the elements appropriately. In this recipe, we'll discuss these new elements and how to properly include them in our app.

Getting ready

Access to an iPad and the **iOS Human Interface Guidelines** will be essential for this recipe. We'll be learning about a few new interface elements, and it will be useful to experience such pieces while we read.

How to do it...

The increased screen size requires new interface elements for several interactions. Some of these changes occur because the larger screen size offers more screen real estate, which can make elements easier to use. Other changes occur because buttons on screen need to get a bit bigger in order to be easily tapped while holding the iPad.

Let's take a look at several interface components that were created or altered for the iPad.

- ▸ Popover
- ▸ A streamlined Toolbar and Navigation Bar
- ▸ Larger Tab Bar
- ▸ Page and form sheets

Each of these interface elements use the larger screen of the iPad to offer increased application capability. Through the rework of existing elements and creation of entirely new elements, Apple's designed quality standard interface elements that will help us create outstanding tablet applications.

How it works...

The larger display of the iPad required new interface elements, as it quickly became obvious that the new device could not simply scale up all previous iOS elements. New pieces such as the Popover would be necessary in order to provide the best possible experience.

The **Popover** is the first new design element, appearing as a variable length window for the placement of different action items or data cells. A Popover for the *App Store* app can be seen in the next screenshot:

We can place a good variety of content inside the Popover. Like nearly every interface element, there are several rules that we must abide by though. The Popover must always lay on top of all other views, a tiny arrow is included to indicate the button that the view originated from, and the Popover must be dismissed when the user taps anywhere in the application outside of the overlay view.

We can use the Popover for almost anything and we're given the ability to include **Tab Bars**, **Navigation Bars**, maps, and pretty much anything else we could imagine. This allows for a good deal of flexibility, essentially giving the ability to create mini applications inside of an app.

Any time we intend on creating an **Action Sheet** inside of our iPad app, it must be presented as a Popover.

Diving into the second point, when on the iPhone, any Navigation Bar or **Toolbar** is relatively limited, often only containing one or two action options for the user. This wasn't due to poor design, but because of a lack of space.

The increase in space allows for greater flexibility and the opportunity for all action tasks to occur though a Toolbar, an experience that Apple calls streamlining. We can use Popovers from these buttons as well, and create a full experience with all app functionality coming from this bar.

Much like the streamlined Toolbar, the Tab Bar also benefits from the increase in screen size. The bar still spans along the bottom of the device's screen, regardless of orientation, containing different tabs that present different views and functions when tapped.

Because of its larger size, we can now include more tabs inside of our Tab Bar. While we're limited to five tabs on the iPhone, we can have as many as seven on the iPad. It's also important to note that while the tabs resize when moving from portrait to landscape view on the iPhone, tabs remain the same size when switching orientation on the iPad.

Finally, when designing something modal on the iPhone, we simply have the content fill up the entire screen in order to take up user focus. However, this method becomes a bit less elegant on the iPad, where we often have no need to fill the entire screen.

Apple's created **Form Sheets** and **Page Sheets** to help solve this problem. Both views are designed to be momentarily present, laying over the app's other functions and forcing the user's attention on the modal task.

Page Sheets have a height that spans the entire device screen and a width equal to that of the iPad, measuring 768 pixels. When in portrait view, a Page Sheet fills the entire screen. If the iPad is being used in landscape view, then there is a slight area where the view below the Page Sheet is visible and dimmed.

A proper Form Sheet can be found in this screenshot of *Mail*. Form Sheets have a constant size of 540 pixels by 620 pixels. This view remains centered on screen unless a keyboard is present, for which the view moves up to be flush with the status bar.

Both views are only possible on the iPad, and work best for modal information where we're presenting information to the user in a linear fashion.

Apple has taken much time in preparation of such special pieces and detailed interface guidelines for each device in order to help developers create the best possible application. The iPad is truly a different computing experience than the iPhone, and the different pieces of the interface will need to behave accordingly.

There's more...

We've just touched the tip of the iceberg with respect to how the iPhone and iPad are different devices. Let's take a further look at other differences between designing for the two devices.

iPad killed the radio star

On the iPhone, video is limited to full-screen display only. So if we're going to include a video in our iPhone app, we have no ability to do anything but make it the sole focus of the user's attention.

For the iPad, we no longer have such a requirement and our video can only take up a small portion of the screen if we so desire. This allows for us to include a video in ways that we never would have before because we feared that it would be too intrusive on the user.

Multi-finger gestures

Apple has created multi-finger gestures that allow for the user to quickly swipe four fingers on screen as a way to move between applications or return to the home screen.

If your application depends upon a four-finger gesture, we may want to find a different way to implement its function. If the user attempts to invoke the action that this gesture links to, they may find themselves inside a different application if they are using iOS 5. This can cause a good deal of confusion, so with Apple's inclusion of this new system-wide gesture in iOS 5, we should work toward phasing out four-finger gestures from our application.

See also

▶ *Migrating our app to the iPad* in this chapter

▶ *Experiences that are possible on the iPad, but not on the iPhone* in this chapter

Designing an app using skeuomorphic designs

Whereas the original iPhone was a novel device unlike anything users had seen before, the iPad brings out a somewhat different initial impression.

In specific, the iPad isn't unlike favorite non-digital devices in many respects. It shares many size and shape characteristics with books, maps, television screens, day calendars, printed photos, and much more.

Because the iPad can mimic physical items much differently than the iPhone and iPod touch, we should consider this fact when designing our interface.

In this recipe we'll discuss **skeuomorphic designs**, which are digital interfaces that resemble a physical item that performs the same task as the application.

Getting ready

Ideally, we will have an iPad on hand with several good examples of quality skeuomorphic applications. Some examples include *iBooks*, *Notes*, *Calendar*, and *Contacts*.

How to do it...

The larger device size of the iPad lends itself to more opportunities for a skeuomorphic interface design. For many applications, the iPad application will be serving to replace an actual physical element such as a book, so there will be an expectation for our work to function like its real life counterpart.

It is quite difficult to create a successful interface that is skeuomorphic and mimics a physical object. It's fairly easy to create something that behaves too realistically, which ends up doing more damage than good to our app's usability.

Let's take a look at several keys to creating a good application interface that is instantly familiar and also intuitive to the first-time user:

- ▸ Our app should not be skeuomorphic for the sake of visuals only
- ▸ Obvious, common actions should perform true to their physical counterparts
- ▸ We should never withhold functionality because it doesn't appear in the physical object

iPad users will appreciate our attempt to create applications that best resemble objects that they're familiar with in real life. If we go about working these tips into our app, we'll be well on our way toward creating a strong skeuomorphic design.

How it works...

The iPad provides a truly unique experience, in the sense that it's thinner and lighter than most books, with a large digital screen that can display attractive art for any application.

In many ways, it provides the power of computing that people have become accustomed to over the past 25 years and allows that power to better mimic traditional physical items in a way never before possible. While traditional computers could never truly replicate a book, drum set, notebook, map, or newspaper, the iPad can. This creates a drastic shift in how people experience the world and intake information, and we can help ease this transition by creating interfaces that seem familiar to the user.

Skeuomorphic designs are a replication of a physical object for the sake of making our design immediately familiar to the user. If we're making an **eBook**, it makes sense to have our application resemble an actual book. The user will immediately know the purpose of our application and how it functions.

If we're going to use a skeuomorphic design, our interface should resemble the physical object in both appearance and behavior. *iBooks* is a great example, where the application mimics the appearance of a physical book, and the user navigates through pages by flicking their finger on screen much like one would grab and turn a paper page as well.

This doesn't require us to only use true to life actions, as an app like *iBooks* also allows for the user to tap the side of the screen to flip between pages as well. But by allowing users to swipe to turn pages, it's simple to provide an easily understood control style with no actual buttons or tutorial because the application behaves exactly like paper books that all users are familiar with.

Continuing on to the idea of common actions acting like their physical counterparts, there are many small decisions that we can make that will help our app perform better. Pretend that we're looking to design an application that downloads and plays top **podcasts** from across the web. For our interface, we may decide to differentiate our work by creating a fun design that mimics a 1980s style radio. The app screen will contain standard components on a real radio from the era, such as a volume knob or tape deck.

If we decide to use such a skeuomorphic design, then these artistic components should behave much like we would expect a real radio to perform. Tapping the volume button should present the user with a way to raise or lower the audio level and pressing upon the tape deck should present the user with a Popover or form sheet that allows for selection of a new podcast.

The user will first look at these graphical locations in our app when they desire to perform a specific action, so they should perform accordingly. It doesn't make sense for our app to look like a radio if it's not going to function like an actual radio, so we should constantly be aware of this when creating our work.

Finally, if we're serious about creating a true-to-life application experience, it makes sense to limit our app to a feature set that stays true to the real life object as well.

For example, if we're creating a notebook application such as Apple's *Notes*, we may want to create an artistic design that mimics a legal pad or small pocket notebook.

The resulting aesthetic definitely provides a skeuomorphic experience, with us maybe even going as far as to include ruled lines and use a font that resembles handwriting. So if we want to give a complete experience, it would make sense to not include features such as e-mail note exporting or search, since these features could never be found on a physical notebook.

However, we should never withhold features for the sake of realism, even if it seems difficult to include the function while keeping within the theme. We should use this challenge to drive creativity, creating a unique way to imagine how features possible with the iPad would behave if plausible in real life. For example, it would never be possible to simply glance through a shelf of books and be able to search the contents of all available books to find a desired passage, yet Apple included a simple search bar in *iBooks* that looks as if it is engraved into the wood bookcase, as showcased in the next screenshot:

iBooks - © 2011 Apple Inc.

This simple, elegant solution offers a powerful tool that isn't possible with a physical bookshelf, yet fits in with a desired artistic theme. Such inclusions aren't always as easy or obvious, but they are greatly appreciated by the user. These subtleties help make the transition from physical item to digital application an easy cognitive process for the user while also creating an attractive art design.

These are just a few tips on different skeuomorphic designs, but with a bit of creativity, we can pull from the user's physical expectations and create an application that is immediately recognizable.

See also

▸ *Migrating our app to the iPad* in this chapter

The Importance of
Direct Manipulation

Without tactile feedback for a button press, users will be looking to other cues for confirmation that an interaction has occurred correctly. As user interface designers, it is our job to make sure that it is clear to the user when they've properly navigated through our application.

This feedback can occur in a variety of situations, be it when pressing upon the Tab Bar, when manipulating a photo, or when flicking through a list. Because our applications run on a touch screen, it's important that we provide proper visual feedback nearly every time the user makes contact with the screen.

Visual feedback is most common, but auditory response is also possible in our application as well. Let's look at how to use these functions to properly provide feedback and indicate to the user that the application is working correctly. By creating clarity for our users, we'll create a better application that will gain higher reviews and minimize confusion.

Giving the user feedback

We've spent time discussing different possible gestures in iOS, such as the pinch or swipe, which will help up determine which interaction is best suited for the activity at hand when developing our application. However, it is not enough to only implement the correct gesture type, as we should also provide adequate visual feedback to the user to help give visual confirmation of the action.

When working in a traditional computer environment, visual feedback is still important; however the user still has a tactile input device to fall back upon. If we're using a keyboard to type in a word processor and the program does not respond instantaneously, we still have the physical press of the key to reinforce that our action was properly performed.

A delay or pause between press of the keyboard and display of the character on screen can cause frustration for the user, but this action is unlikely to cause confusion. In tapping the keyboard, we reaffirm that we've hit the key correctly and a delay or failure to display the pressed key indicates that either the software is working improperly or there has been a hardware error. There is little uncertainty and with this knowledge, the user has some insight as to why the problem has occurred.

However, once we move to the touch screen, visual feedback becomes absolutely vital, as it serves as the primary method for showing the user that an interface element was touched correctly. Much like a word processor that doesn't register keystrokes, a touch interface that doesn't provide some sort of visual feedback can be a frustrating experience. But whereas our keyboard provides tactile confirmation upon pressing the key, we have no such luxury when working with a piece of glass on the iPhone.

If we fail to provide some sort of feedback, users will have little to fall back on and explain the error. Did the user miss the button with their finger? Is the application in some sort of processing state that doesn't allow the button to be pressed? Is the button that the user is attempting to tap actually a button? These are just several questions that arise when improper visual feedback is given.

Providing visual response to a tap or shake isn't enough though, as this reaction must also occur without any sense of delay to the user. In applications like Apple's Photos, where images can be zoomed in or out on with a pinch, it is essential that apparent changes occur so that the users can recognize the action as well to allow for precise manipulation. Take an iPhone or iPad at hand and open the *Photos* or *Safari* app. While pinching in and out to pan the zoom, it is easy to understand the need for immediate visual reaction from our application.

If an iPhone were to take even an extra second after the pinch to properly proportion the newly sized image, the delay would cause frustration, as the user would need to wait for the photo to reappear on screen before knowing if the zoom level is acceptable. If the image is pinched in a bit too far, the user would then have to adjust the photo, wait for the picture to appear resized, and repeat this process again until the image is satisfactory.

Apple has solved a good portion of our problems for us with all standard system interface elements, which help to make our job easier. If we implement the standard Tab Bar, Navigation Bar, or Scroll View, our interface design will already perform basic and expected actions to visually aid a user. If we're still uncomfortable with producing acceptable feedback to the user, we should reply upon Apple's standard interface elements as much as possible. So long as we stay with established standards like those found in the Interface Builder, we should at least provide a minimal required level of visual affirmation.

Visual feedback will become much more difficult once we begin to design custom application elements. When creating these non-standard buttons, sliders, or navigation elements we should proceed with extreme caution. In many situations, we can create a great deal of confusion and difficulty for our user by creating a custom navigation or interaction element, mostly due to the fact that visual feedback will not respond as expected for the user.

If we do design to step outside Apple's provided interface elements, we should look around iOS for inspiration on how our applications should respond to taps or swipes. Tapping on icons or a button provides a quick shaded overlay that acknowledges the press. When sliding the volume control in the iPod app, the representative slider quickly keeps up with our finger. Rotating an iPad from portrait to landscape view provides a smooth animation to help our brain comprehend the shift in perspective. In many applications, a loading wheel will spin to help signify that a task is currently processing and holding up the device temporarily. These responses are a mere sampling of how iOS responds to various interactions, and implementing a custom interface design; we should look to corresponding features in iOS which most closely mimic what we're attempting to build for guidance.

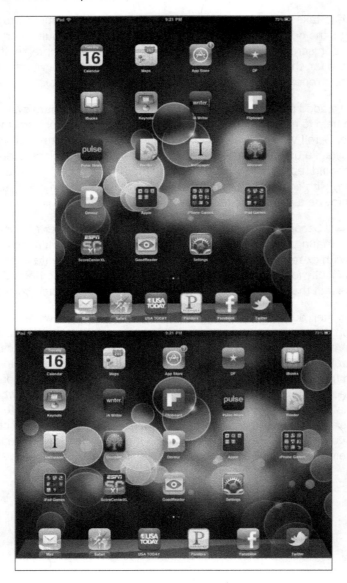

Audio clues can work to provide equal aid to the user as well and are often neglected when building an interface. For several examples of sound response in iOS, we can find that tapping the pause or play controls on the *iPod* application will quickly start a song or a quick chime will accompany a new e-mail. Likewise, game applications often make use of short sound effects to signal that a character has jumped or a weapon has fired.

When looking to implement sound into our applications, we should refrain from excessively loud or startling sounds. Our auditory clues should be soft, subtle, and provide adequate confirmation while not intruding upon our user.

Visual and auditory clues are greatly important for the success of our app, as there is no other sense of possible feedback and users will rely upon such notifications.

Many influential and inspiring books have been written on the topic of human interface design and how the human brain psychologically breaks down and interprets information presented on a computer screen. Here are a few suggested books to read up on for more information on the subject.

- Written by the father of the Macintosh, Jef Raskin, The Humane Interface (ISBN-13: 978-0201379372) is a masterpiece on user experience and interface design. Raskin dives into great length on a variety of meaningful topics and is able to simplify complex areas of cognitive research into simple lessons on creating better applications for the end user.

- *How to Think Like a Great Graphic Designer* by Debbie Millman (ISBN-13: 978-1581154962) is a collection of 20 interviews with renowned designers, focusing on a variety of problems similar to what we'll be fighting everyday. It's a great book of insight into the lives of the best designers in the business.

If you need a stylus, you blew it

When questioned about input methods on the iPad, former Apple CEO Steve Jobs offered up one of his most quote-worthy quips in recent memory, telling journalists about competitors, "If you see a stylus, they blew it." Throughout the life of iOS, Apple has taken the strong stance that mobile computing should remain an exercise best fit for the fingertips.

Steve Jobs was a remarkable CEO and public speaker. His keynotes on iOS were often an interesting public display of the operating system and a must-watch for any developer. Apple makes public all keynotes as a podcast, in case we haven't seen them, at `http://itunes.apple.com/podcast/id275834665`.

We've already discussed the importance of understanding the difference between the portrait and landscape perspectives with regards to how users hold the device in their hands, but what about the differences between a finger and a mouse as a pointing device?

In developing an interface for the iOS, it is important to understand the fundamental differences between the mouse pointer and the pointer finger. In this appendix, we'll discuss several of the physical and philosophical differences between the two pointing devices.

While touch screen displays have become quite commonplace, the introduction of the iPhone in 2007 signaled the beginning of a new generation of mobile devices by ditching a keyboard altogether. At the time, the world had yet to see a finger focused mobile device that worked well and many were skeptical.

Apple differentiated from competitors and predecessors in two distinct ways when building the iPhone, which helped vault the device to success. First, Apple backed away from the notion that a **stylus** was required for successful touch interaction. Second, much thought was put into designing an attentive operating system that reacts quickly and obviously to touch inputs.

The loss of the stylus was seen as a way to break the physical barrier between human and computer in a mobile environment. For millions, the iPhone was the first available **capacitive touch screen** experience which was accurate enough to not require a stylus. The detachment from a stylus or keyboard can be a detriment in some situations, as it also takes away the ability for tactile user feedback. With iOS, the finger became the direct input device responsible for tapping the screen.

In contrasting the differences between a **click** and a **tap**, there are three distinct attributes on which we should focus our attention: speed of a touch or click, radius of a touch or click, and the speed at which the user can move from one side of the screen to the other.

Speed is inherently different between devices due to the physical act required to perform either a double tap or a double click. Pick up a mouse to perform a quick double click upon a file and consciously make an effort to notice the motion of clicking. Computer mice are designed to make the click as simple and comfortable as possible, so it shouldn't be a surprise to us that the double click has become a common action for file selection. The mouse also has the benefit of being detached from the computer, which allows for relative 2D motion as interpreted by a device sitting on a table next to the computer monitor. Our pointer finger can remain on the mouse at all times, which allows us to perform a double tap at moments notice.

In contrast, iOS devices are designed so that fingers do not make unintentional contact with the interface while being held with our hands. The iPhone and iPod touch lay flush in a palm while the iPad contains a bezel that measures nearly one inch in width. In order to use our pointer finger to tap upon the iOS screen, we must hold the device in one hand and then extend our other hand and make contact with the screen. This pointing dilemma is one of the driving reasons as to why the **Tab Bar** view controller works so well on the iPhone, as the placement of the bar on the bottom of the screen allows for easy reach with the thumb of the hand holding the device.

 Keeping this attribute in mind, we should focus on keeping tap sensitive elements to a minimum and within reach of the thumb from the hand holding the device when possible.

As we can see in the next screenshot, important elements on screen are placed to be within a quick thumb tap:

Radius is another important component of successful interface design. Unfortunately, the human body did not evolve with touch screens in mind and we are left carrying relatively large fingers with inherent computer interaction flaws.

The width of a finger is the most difficult obstacle, as radius of a tap can vary from person to person. As such, we must plan for large fingers with every interface we build, which can take up a great deal of space. Apple suggests that interface items be of a size at least equal to **44 pixels by 44 pixels**, which equates to an 88 pixel square on the Retina Display. At this size, the average tap is equal to nearly 14 percent of the width of the screen and 9 percent of the height, which is a considerable chunk of real estate.

 For means of comparison, on a 320 x 480 pixels iPhone or iPod touch screen, the Navigation Bar measures 44 pixels tall and the Tab Bar measures 49 pixels tall, numbers that fit accordingly with Apple's recommendation that interface elements measure at least 44 x 44 pixels for easy interaction.

While fingertips are taking up a considerable portion of our real estate, we haven't even begun to calculate lost real estate from the rest of our finger that acts as an obtrusion to the screen under it.

If we place our finger on the top half of an iPhone screen, we'll quickly see that the tapping finger covers a great portion of the screen. Again, this is lost interface space during the moment that a tap occurs and we should design our interfaces with this flaw in mind. If when interacting with an interface element on screen, it is required that a user also have access to information located below that element, conflict will arise and important data will be rendered inaccessible. In the next image, we can see an example of such data loss:

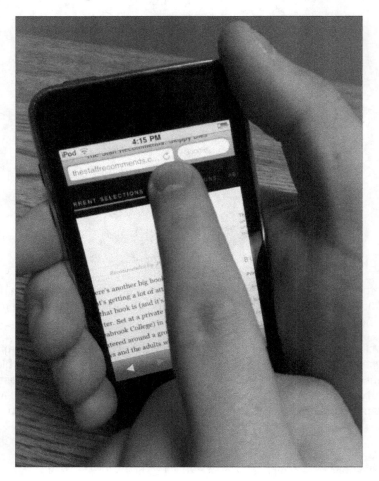

If we compare the radius of a touch to the click of a mouse, we see the drastic differences in size and clarity. Mouse pointers are designed to be small in size, where a slight movement of our mouse on a 2D plane on our desk corresponding with an equally slight movement on screen. Scrolling speeds, momentum, and other speed attributes can be customized in software, allowing a unique experience between users. Because mouse movement occurs on a separate device, traditional computer interfaces also need not worry about ever having the mouse pointer block important information on screen.

Finally, the speed at which a user can scan across and interact with two different interface items is another important challenge with our interface. When using a mouse, quick shifts from one side of the screen to the other are simple. A sudden movement of the mouse on the desk can easily translate into a pointer movement across screen. However, movement across the iPhone or iPad can be quite different. In order to move across the screen, the user must physically pick up their finger, and then place it down upon another part of screen. This interaction is unnatural, uncomfortable, and lengthy.

Fingertips covering up important screen real estate can become problematic with speed as well. If our interface changes drastically after pressing upon a button, the user cannot visually see and react the entire screen until the finger has been lifted. Under a mouse pointer system, the user has the benefit of being able to react instantaneously to changes in an interface. This delay can be most apparent in games and applications that are fast paced, where important information or game characters require quick reaction time for success.

Jumping off a cliff in a platform game or losing important information because it is obscured under a finger can be extremely frustrating to an iOS user and our interface designs should be built to prevent such situations.

The surface isn't always slippery

Due to a **fingerprint protective** coating that Apple uses on most iOS devices, swiping a finger across the screen of an iPhone or iPad can sometimes be met with a frictional resistance.

There isn't a huge sense of force when pushing a finger across screen, but the coating can be noticeable nonetheless. When planning an interface that requires quick swiping, keep this slight resistance in mind as it can sometimes make swiping on screen a bit slow.

This protective coating can slightly vary between device models and can slightly wear out over time as well, which can also affect the level of resistance between finger and screen.

Paying attention to subtle details in each iOS device, like the resistance of the protective coating, can help turn a mediocre app into a spectacular interface.

Index

J

joystick 118
jQTouch
    URL 27

L

local notification
    about 158-161
    controlling 158
location services
    about 168
    using, steps 169
    working 170

M

magazine app icon, Newsstand feature
    optimizing, for Newsstand 56, 57
maps app 13
Matt Rix, blog
    URL 204
Merge Copy tool 59
microphone 119
mobile
    gaming platform 113
    platforms 114
Mobile Human Interface Guidelines
    URL 140
modal views
    Current Context modal view 64
    dual modalities 67
    page curl transition 66
    utilizing 64-67
mouse 236
multi-finger gestures 224
multi-pane method 216, 217
multitasking
    accomodations, making 151-153
    working with 145-147

N

navigation bar
    style, adding 91
    used, for implementing application functional-
       ity 88-91

navigation bar views 10-13
Netflix 205
newspaper app icon, Newsstand feature
    optimizing, for Newsstand 56, 57
Newsstand
    in iOS 5 149-151
Newsstand feature
    magazine app icon, optimizing 56, 57
    newspaper app icon, optimizing 56, 57

P

Pareto principle 180
Penultimate 207
periodical downloads
    in iOS 5 149-151
phone calls 142, 145
pickers
    about 97
    used, for speeding up data entry 95-97
picker views 15
pixel resolution 209
playback 166
popover 220, 222
popovers pane views 10
Provisioning Profile 33
push notification
    about 158-161
    controlling 158
    single button notification, using 161

R

radius 237
rapid prototype
    about 25
    preparing, steps 26, 27
    working 28
raster images 29
ratio changes 208
rear-facing camera 3
record 166
resolution 208
retina display 119
    migrating to 28-31
    working 31, 32
Retina iPad 211
rounded edges effect

[PACKT]
PUBLISHING

Thank you for buying
iPhone User Interface Cookbook

About Packt Publishing

Packt, pronounced 'packed', published its first book "*Mastering phpMyAdmin for Effective MySQL Management*" in April 2004 and subsequently continued to specialize in publishing highly focused books on specific technologies and solutions.

Our books and publications share the experiences of your fellow IT professionals in adapting and customizing today's systems, applications, and frameworks. Our solution based books give you the knowledge and power to customize the software and technologies you're using to get the job done. Packt books are more specific and less general than the IT books you have seen in the past. Our unique business model allows us to bring you more focused information, giving you more of what you need to know, and less of what you don't.

Packt is a modern, yet unique publishing company, which focuses on producing quality, cutting-edge books for communities of developers, administrators, and newbies alike. For more information, please visit our website: www.packtpub.com.

Writing for Packt

We welcome all inquiries from people who are interested in authoring. Book proposals should be sent to author@packtpub.com. If your book idea is still at an early stage and you would like to discuss it first before writing a formal book proposal, contact us; one of our commissioning editors will get in touch with you.

We're not just looking for published authors; if you have strong technical skills but no writing experience, our experienced editors can help you develop a writing career, or simply get some additional reward for your expertise.

iPhone Applications Tune-Up

ISBN: 978-1-84969-034-8   Paperback: 256 pages

High performance tuning guide for real-world iOS projects

1. Tune up every aspect of your iOS application for greater levels of stability and performance

2. Improve the users' experience by boosting the performance of your app

3. Learn to use Xcode's powerful native features to increase productivity

4. Profile and measure every operation of your application for performance

iPhone JavaScript Cookbook

ISBN: 978-1-84969-108-6   Paperback: 328 pages

Clear and practical recipes for building web applications using JavaScript and AJAX without having to learn Objective-C or Cocoa

1. Build web applications for iPhone with a native look feel using only JavaScript, CSS, and XHTML

2. Develop applications faster using frameworks

3. Integrate videos, sound, and images into your iPhone applications

4. Write code to integrate your own applications with famous websites such as Facebook, Twitter, and Flickr

Please check **www.PacktPub.com** for information on our titles

Xcode 4 iOS Development Beginner's Guide

ISBN: 978-1-84969-130-7   Paperback: 432 pages

Use the powerful Xcode 4 suite of tools to build applications for the iPhone and iPad from scratch

1. Learn how to use Xcode 4 to build simple, yet powerful applications with ease

2. Each chapter builds on what you have learned already

3. Learn to add audio and video playback to your applications

4. Plentiful step-by-step examples, images, and diagrams to get you up to speed in no time with helpful hints along the way

iAd Production Beginner's Guide: RAW

ISBN: 978-1-84969-132-1   Paperback: 435 pages

Create motion-rich, beautiful iAd adverts for iOS devices and incorporate techniques to help boost revenue and brand awareness

1. Create interactive iAd mobile adverts that appear in applications downloaded from the App Store

2. Learn to use the drag and drop visual tool, iAd Producer, to create ads without any experience with the underlying technologies

3. Reach an audience that downloads over 200 apps per second and leave a lasting, memorable image of your brand with rich immersive ads

www.ingramcontent.com/pod-product-compliance
Lightning Source LLC
LaVergne TN
LVHW062312060326
832902LV00013B/2165